W9-ADF-024

THE HODDER COMPENDIUM
OF CHRISTIAN CURIOSITIES

The Hodder Compendium of CHRISTIAN CURIOSITIES

DAVID MOLONEY

**HODDER &
STOUGHTON**

Unless indicated otherwise, Scripture quotations are taken from the
Holy Bible, New International Version.
Copyright © 1973, 1978, 1984 by International Bible Society.
Used by permission. All rights reserved.

First published in Great Britain in 2008 by Hodder & Stoughton
An Hachette Livre UK company

1

Copyright © David Moloney 2008

The right of David Moloney to be identified as the Author of the Work has been
asserted by him in accordance with the Copyright, Designs and Patents Act 1988.

All rights reserved. No part of this publication may be reproduced, stored in a
retrieval system, or transmitted, in any form or by any means without the prior
written permission of the publisher, nor be otherwise circulated in any form of
binding or cover other than that in which it is published and without a similar
condition being imposed on the subsequent purchaser.

A CIP catalogue record for this title is available from the British Library

ISBN 978 0 340 97922 8

Typeset in Filosophia

Book design by Janette Revill
Printed and bound by Clays Ltd, St Ives plc

Hodder & Stoughton policy is to use papers that are natural, renewable
and recyclable products and made from wood grown in sustainable forests.
The logging and manufacturing processes are expected to conform to the
environmental regulations of the country of origin.

Hodder & Stoughton Ltd
338 Euston Road
London NW1 3BH

www.hodderfaith.com

⁎⦃ DEDICATION ⦃⁎

'That's what you need.'
Roy Castle

Charmian Allwright, Lucy Avery, Jaimee Biggins, Loreen Brown, Charlotte Collingwood, Beatrice Cook, Tanya Cowell, Jamie Cowen, Jo Davey, Jenny Davis, Sarah Dennis, Jessica Dixon, Alex Dury, Renaud Edvardsen, Louise Edwards, Victoria Fedorowicz, Alex Garside, Sarah Giles, Eleanor Goody, Jo Gravestock, Meg Greatrex, Wendy Grisham, Elizabeth Hallett, Julie Hatherall, Lyndal Hayward, Kate Hibbert, Mary Houghton, Ngan Ho, Jamie Hodder-Williams, Ozden Isik, Lorraine Keating, Suzanne Kennedy, Patrick Knowles, Hannah Little, Judith Longman, Abigail Lucas, Ian Metcalfe, Cecilia Moore, Tim Moyler, Martin Mullin, Martin Neild, Charles Nettleton, Kate O'Hearn, Claire Portal, Kathryn Pritchard, Abigail Ratcliffe, Mark Read, Emma Redfern, Annabel Robson, Rebecca Russel-Ponte, Helen Sampson, Adam Sofianos, Kevin Stewart, Mary Tapissier, Catriona Taylor, Allyson Thomas, Zelda Turner, Suzy Van Den Berg, Katherine Venn, Paul Walker, Liz Ward, Rachel Welch, Helen Windrath, Jean Whitnall, Viv Wickham, Brett Woods, Denise Woolery … a ten-year compendium of Hodder curious Christians.

⟩ contents ⟨

'Godliness with contentment is great gain.'
1 Timothy 6:6

⟩ INTRODUCTION ⟨

'"Curiouser and Curiouser!" cried Alice.'
Lewis Carroll

I 'became' a Christian – in that I got down on my knees and asked
Jesus to come into my life, using the words that several Christian
friends had told me I should – shortly before my eighteenth
birthday in a hotel next to Chartres Cathedral in France, at the
beginning of a family holiday. It had taken me a long time to find
the courage to pray that prayer, mainly because I wasn't really sure
why I should. My friends had given me plenty of reasons: I would
be saved, and go to heaven; I would be filled with the Holy Spirit,
and 'never be bored again'; everything in the Bible was literal
truth, and I had a duty to respond; Jesus, through some complicated system of atonement, had died so that I might be forgiven
for my sins. But, while I could see the logic in these arguments,
they were never quite enough to convince me to commit myself to
this hard-and-fast belief system. They were a little too abstract
and intellectual and I've always been a heart person, not a head
person.

But something happened to me in Chartres. It was something
to do with the cathedral. I remember the impression it made on
me before we even reached the city – it dominates the flat surrounding countryside like a huge ocean liner, and captured my
attention from several miles away. Once we had arrived and
booked into our hotel, we toured the cathedral and I was captivat-
ed by the dark, beautiful, Gothic immenseness of this fantastic
building: its heavy, solid walls with dominating flying buttresses,
its intimidating west façade with dramatic rose window and its
two, soaring, non-symmetrical spires, all covered with intricate
sculptures and gargoyles. I was thrilled by the sheer scale, the
workmanship, the detail, the imagination, the adventure of the
place. This incredible building was created by men, and for what

purpose? In honour of something magnificent – a monument to God. Now *this* was something worth believing in.

Oh, and I really, *really* fancied a girl in the local church back home.

I never got the girl, but I did spend a lot of time with the local church – a lively charismatic house church – over the next year. The people there were all very committed, warm, Bible-believing Christians and they made me feel part of a close-knit church family. Then I went to university, and started a career, and the world opened up for me – I met Christians from other traditions and made very close friendships with people of no particular faith at all. My worldview changed and I became less comfortable with the very conservative, certain teaching of the church at home. I grew disaffected with the modern-day Church – it seemed to me that it was concerned only with being *relevant*, culturally and intellectually acceptable to the rest of the world. I lost sight of what it was that attracted me to faith in the first place – something deep, stirring and mysterious, something creative and human but reaching out to something magnificent and untouchable.

But my first years as a Christian had given me a sense of faith and a confidence to talk to God which I think will always remain with me, and it also redirected the path of my life deeper inside the universe and culture of Christianity. Gradually, I think I'm starting to rediscover some of those touchstones in our world that connect us with God and reaffirm our faith – what my favourite Christian author Philip Yancey calls 'rumours of another world'. It's where I now make my living – publishing Christian books – and it is a universe of which I have tried to capture the essence in this compendium.

Christianity is two thousand years old. It has over two billion living adherents – almost a third of the population of the world – and new believers of all traditions and denominations are born into the faith every day. It is infinitely diverse. It is rich, historic, eccentric. It has produced art, pronouncements and acts of wisdom and beauty. It has also produced immense horrors and embarrassments. It is human – that is what humans do, unfortunately. But I believe the humanity of the Church – the failures that accompany the successes, and the humour that accompanies the grit – is what makes it most attractive, and believable. It's when we try to pretend that we are something we're not that the rest of the world gets suspicious and irritated.

The Hodder Compendium of Christian Curiosities attempts to show what is great and what is not so great about Christianity. Whatever your beliefs, if you have a curious mind there should be something in here to interest you.

David Moloney

✻} number crunching {✻

Christianity is by some distance the world's largest religion, in terms of practising adherents, as the following figures published in 2007 show. Whatever your thoughts on religion, and Christianity in particular, its significance in the world we live in today cannot be ignored.

AFRICA

Christians	432,553,000
Roman Catholic	151,951,000
Protestant	121,917,000
Independent	93,100,000
Muslims	368,116,300
Ethnic Religions	112,254,000
Hindus	2,749,000
Baha'is	2,103,000

EUROPE

Christians	556,284,600
Roman Catholic	278,870,000
Orthodox	158,220,000
Protestant	70,995,000
Muslims	33,260,800
Jews	2,017,000
Buddhists	1,645,000
Hindus	1,478,000

ASIA

Muslims	927,077,000
Hindus	865,072,000
Chinese Universists	385,284,000
Buddhists	376,365,000
Christians	354,444,000
Independent	186,844,000
Roman Catholic	126,256,000
Protestant	58,788,000

LATIN AMERICA

Christians	526,632,700
Roman Catholic	489,356,000
Protestant	56,613,000
Independent	45,031,000
Spiritists	13,033,000
Ethnic Religions	3,501,000
Muslims	1,758,000
Jews	1,237,000

NORTH AMERICA

Christians	276,490,800
Independent	80,643,000
Roman Catholic	80,620,000
Protestant	66,035,000
Jews	6,169,000
Muslims	5,334,600
Buddhists	3,142,000
Hindus	1,490,000

OCEANIA

Christians	26,778,300
Roman Catholic	8,676,000
Protestant	7,841,000
Anglican	4,953,000
Buddhists	506,000
Hindus	424,000
Muslims	417,000
Ethnic Religions	318,000

WORLD

Christians	2,173,183,400
Roman Catholic	1,135,729,000
Independent	432,223,000
Protestant	382,179,000
Muslims	1,335,964,100
Hindus	871,982,000
Chinese Universists	386,666,900
Buddhists	382,542,000
Jews	263,840,000

Note: These figures are as listed in the *2007 Encyclopedia Britannica Book of the Year*, which differentiates between Protestant and Anglican denominations. Independent refers to members of churches which regard themselves independent from historic church traditions. Chinese Universism includes followers of all Chinese folk religions. For each major continent or land mass, I have listed the five largest religions and, under Christianity in each section, the three largest denominations.

✳{ THE WORD FOR ALL }✳

'Go and make disciples of all nations,' commanded Jesus before he ascended to heaven. These fascinating statistics from Wycliffe International, the Bible translation agency, reveal the size of the challenge of making the gospel available to all.

2,251 languages do not have a translation of the Bible; that's just under 33 per cent of the 6,912 languages spoken in the world today.

438 language communities have access to the complete Bible in the language they know best.

193,000,000 people speak the languages without a translation of the Bible; that's 3 per cent of the population of the world.

Almost 80 per cent of these languages are spoken in three areas of the world: Central Africa and Nigeria (over 500 languages), mainland and Southeast Asia (over 500 languages) and Indonesia and the Pacific Islands (750 languages).

1,953 translation programmes are currently underway for languages without adequate Bible translations. Wycliffe Bible translators aim to have started a programme in every single language that needs one by the year 2025.

Note: statistics apply to 2007.

✳﴿ TEN DESCRIPTIONS OF GOD ﴾✳

God has many attributes and the Bible is packed with descriptions that help us understand him better.

TEACHER
'You call me "Teacher" and "Lord", and rightly so, for that is what I am.'
John 13:14

SHEPHERD
'The LORD is my shepherd, I shall not be in want.'
Psalm 23:1

ROCK
'The LORD is my rock, my fortress and my deliverer; my God is my rock, in whom I take refuge.'
Psalm 18:2

HUSBAND
'For your Maker is your husband – the LORD Almighty is his name.'
Isaiah 54:5

WARRIOR
'The LORD is a warrior; the LORD is his name.'
Exodus 15:3

THE EYE OF THE STORM
'Our God comes and will not be silent; a fire devours before him, and around him a tempest rages.'
Psalm 50:3

JUDGE
'O LORD Almighty, you who judge righteously and test the heart and mind.'
Jeremiah 11:20

HEALER
'I will bring health and healing ... I will heal my people and will let them enjoy abundant peace and security.'
Jeremiah 33:6

KING
'Now to the King eternal, immortal, invisible, the only God, be honour and glory for ever and ever.'
1 Timothy 1:17

FATHER
'A father to the fatherless, a defender of widows, is God in his holy dwelling.'
Psalm 68:5

⁕⟩ GREAT MEALS OF THE BIBLE ⟨⁕

*Descriptions of food play a very important role throughout the
Bible. Meals feature at some of the most significant points in the
Old and New Testament narratives, generally with symbolic meaning. They also give us a fascinating insight into the diets, life and
culture of Bible times. Here are ten curious feasts.*

GOD FEEDS MAN

We start the list with possibly the greatest feast ever
laid on for man. 'I give you every seed-bearing plant on
the face of the earth and every tree that has fruit with seed
in it. They will be yours for food,' God told Adam. 'You are
free to eat from any tree in the garden; but you must not
eat from the tree of the knowledge of good and evil, for
when you eat of it you will surely die.' Sadly the temptation
to eat what they shouldn't – a feeling we all know well now
– overcame Adam and Eve.

⊕

MAN FEEDS GOD

How would you feed three uninvited guests,
especially when it turns out they are God himself
and two angels? Abraham pulled out all the stops: he
called for water so his honoured visitors could wash
their feet under the shade of a tree, before feasting on
freshly baked bread of the finest flour, curds and
milk and the meat of a choice, tender calf.

⊕

JACOB'S STEW

They say that food is the way to a man's heart and this was
true for Jacob, who won his father Isaac's inheritance and
deathbed blessing from his older brother Esau over the
course of two meals. Jacob's red lentil stew was so enticing
that Esau traded his birthright for a bowl. In later years,
Jacob disguised himself as his hairier brother and brought
his blind, dying father his favourite dish of goat meat,
claiming for himself the blessing of rule over nations.

⊕

HEAVENLY FOOD

There was unrest borne of hunger among the
Israelites on their long journey to the Promised Land.
Things had been rough as slaves in Egypt, but at least they
always had food to eat – meat and fish, cucumbers, melons,
leeks, onions and garlic. But God sent them a different
kind of feast – hundreds of quail, blown inland by a powerful wind, and the miraculous appearance of *manna*, a
white, wafer-like bread that tasted of honey.

⊕

FEAST FOR A KING

Another example of Old Testament hospitality. When
David and his officials, on the run from his rebellious son
Absalom, arrived at the city of Mahanaim they were given
shelter, bedding and food including wheat and barley,
flour and roasted grain, beans and lentils, honey and
curds, sheep and cheese.

THE KINDNESS OF STRANGERS

The widow of Zarephath believed she had only enough
flour and oil to make one final meal for herself and her
son. When she made a bread cake for the prophet Elijah
instead, God blessed her with a jar of flour that never
emptied and a jug of oil that never ran dry.

THE WILD MAN OF THE DESERT

John the Baptist wore clothes of rough camel hair.
He operated out in the desert, baptising and firebrand
preaching against the religious leaders of the day. And he
ate locusts and wild honey. Some studies have suggested it
is unlikely he survived in the desert on these alone – while
locusts or grasshoppers and uncultivated honey would
provide a rich source of protein and calories, there would
be precious few carbohydrates and virtually no vitamin C,
creating a severe risk that John would contract scurvy.

FEEDING OF THE FIVE THOUSAND

One of Jesus' best-known miracles, he commanded
his disciples to take five loaves of bread and two
fish from which they managed to feed and satisfy around
five thousand people, and fill twelve baskets full of
remains afterwards.

THE LAST SUPPER

At the start of the Festival of Unleavened Bread, Jesus
sat down with his twelve disciples for the Passover meal.
The meal marked the beginning of the Jewish people's
commemoration of the liberation of the Israelites from
slavery, but Jesus gave this particular meal a whole new
meaning for those who accepted him as the Messiah when
he took the bread, gave thanks and broke it, and gave it to
his disciples to eat, telling them it was his body, then
passed around a cup of wine, telling them it was his blood
and marked the new covenant which his death would
establish between people and God.

⊕

A PIECE OF FISH

When Jesus reappeared to his disciples after his resurrection, he compounded their astonishment by asking for
something to eat. They gave him a piece of broiled fish
which he ate as they watched, demonstrating that he was
more than some spiritual apparition but as real and physi-
cally present as any of them. Some translations of the Bible
say they gave him some honeycomb as well as the fish.

⁂⟨ RELICS OF THE SAINTS ⟩⁑

In Christian terms, relics are either the material remains of a saint after his or her death, or sacred objects that have been in contact with the saint's body. There have always been branches of the Church that have held relics in high veneration, although the belief that there is supernatural power in inanimate objects is vulnerable to abuse and the Middle Ages saw thousands of fake relics imported to Europe from the Holy Land.

The Roman Catholic Church has a classification system for the inherent importance and power of relics:

1ˢᵀ-CLASS RELICS

Items directly associated with the events of Christ's life, or the physical remains of a saint. Examples include the Turin Shroud, or the bones of Elisha.

2ᴺᴰ-CLASS RELICS

An item owned, worn or used by a saint. For example, the handkerchiefs that Paul touched while in Ephesus, or the chains of Peter.

3ᴿᴰ-CLASS RELICS

Anything that has touched a first- or second-class relic, resulting in the transference of some of its sacred power. Third-class relics are most often pieces of cloth, and a healthy (or not so healthy, depending on your point of view) trade of such fragments, attached to the back of medals and pendants, continues today on the internet.

✵⁅ common and uncommon denominations ⁆✵

This table lists the approximate foundation date of most of the major bodies, denominations and movements in Christianity. Those in small caps are distant cousins – movements related to Christianity whose central theology is significantly removed from the teaching of orthodox trinitarian belief. For curiosity's sake, the foundation dates of major non-Christian religions are also included in italics.

1500–500 BC	*Vedic religions/Hinduism*
11th Century BC	*Judaism. The Israelites receive the Torah*
9th Century BC	*Jainism*
6th Century BC	*Buddhism*
AD c.30	Christianity.
107	First known use of the term 'Catholic Church'
451	Oriental Orthodoxy
610	*Islam*
1054	Roman Catholic Church/Eastern Orthodox Church.
1469	*Sikhism*
1534	Anglican Communion
1560	Presbyterianism
1565	UNITARIAN CHRISTIANITY
1648	RELIGIOUS SOCIETY OF FRIENDS (QUAKERS)
1693	Amish
1708	Brethren

1727	Moravian Church
1784	Methodist Church
1789	Episcopal Church
1830	CHURCH OF JESUS CHRIST OF LATTER-DAY SAINTS (MORMONS)
1845	CHRISTADELPHIANS
1845	Southern Baptist Convention
1863	*Baha'i Faith*
1863	Seventh-day Adventist Church
1865	Salvation Army
1870	JEHOVAH'S WITNESSES
1879	CHRISTIAN SCIENTISTS
1902	*Liberal Judaism*
1913	*Conservative Judaism*
1914	ASSEMBLIES OF GOD
1931	*Nation of Islam*
1951	*Wicca*
1954	UNIFICATION CHURCH (MOONIES)
1954	*Church of Scientology*
1977	*Jedi*

❧ DO GEESE SEE GOD? ❧

Christians have always placed great store in the power of words so it is unsurprising – but not unfascinating – to discover a Christian seam of palindromes: those rare sentences and phrases which read exactly the same backwards as forwards.

NIYON ANOMHMATA MH MONAN OYIN

This Greek inscription, meaning 'Cleanse my sins and not my face only' can be found on the fonts of seventeen churches in England.

✛

MADAM IN EDEN, I'M ADAM

The first ever chat-up line, to which the palindromic madam might have replied shyly: 'EVE', rudely: 'EVE, MAD ADAM, EVE!', or obscurely: 'NAME NO ONE MAN'.

✛

SO MAY OBADIAH, EVEN IN NINEVEH AID A BOY, AMOS

A popular Christian palindrome, although it makes little sense, even with EVEN IN NINEVEH removed.

✛

SATOR AREPO TENET OPERA ROTAS

This is a Latin palindrome, possibly translating as 'The sower Arepo holds the wheels with effort', which can be arranged as a square so the same phrase can be read in all directions, from left to right, top to bottom, right to left and bottom to top:

```
S A T O R
A R E P O
T E N E T
O P E R A
R O T A S
```

The 'Sator Square' becomes even more curious if each of the letters is ascribed a numeric value (A=1 and Z=26). The total value of each word would then be 73, 55, 64, 55 and 73 – all numbers whose individual digits add up to ten. Some numerologists claim this gives the square extraordinary powers.

Although earliest discoveries of the square predate Christianity, it is believed to have been adopted by early Christians as a secret sign in cities where they faced persecution. The letters can be rearranged in a cross to read PATER NOSTER, Latin for 'Our Father', while the remaining A's and the O's symbolise God as the Alpha and Omega:

```
                    P
                    A
        A           T           O
                    E
                    R
    P A T E R   N O S T E R
                    O
                    S
        O           T           A
                    E
                    R
```

Another interpretation of the Sator Square is to read it in alternating directions, with the central word TENET repeated, so: SATOR OPERA TENET; TENET OPERA SATOR, which could be translated as 'The Great Sower holds in his hand all works; all works the Great Sower holds in his hand.'

✣

SHALL WE ALL DIE?
WE SHALL DIE ALL;
ALL DIE SHALL WE –
DIE ALL WE SHALL.

This cheery epitaph – a word-unit palindrome rather than a pure palindrome – is inscribed in the graveyard at St Winwalloe's Church, in Gunwalloe, Cornwall.

✣

DID I DO, O GOD? DID I AS I SAID I'D DO?
GOOD, I DID!

A happier, if over-anxious, epitaph.

⁂{ BEASTS OF LAND, SEA AND SKY }⁂

Over one hundred species of animal are mentioned in the Bible, and often play surprising roles in events. Here are ten of the more curiously referenced creatures.

✣ SERPENT
The devil's first appearance on earth was in the guise of a serpent. As part of his punishment for deceiving Adam and Eve, he was cursed to 'crawl on his belly' all of his life. Does this mean he was walking prior to the event?

✣ DOVES
A bird of great importance in the Bible. After forty days sailing the flooded earth, Noah sent a dove to find out if the waters were receding. Over two thousand years later, the baptism of Jesus is marked by the Holy Spirit, in the form of a dove, descending from heaven and alighting on him.

✣ DONKEYS
The 'little donkey' who carried Mary and her heavy load along the dusty road to Bethlehem has become an unlikely hero of the faith, but there is no mention of it in any of the Gospel accounts of Jesus' birth. 'Balaam's Ass' is a less well-known biblical donkey from the book of Numbers – she

wisely refused to carry Balaam past a sword-carrying angel. When Balaam beat her, God gave the poor beast the power of speech and she gave her rider an earful of donkey gripe.

✣ PIGS
Jesus cast the evil spirits from two violent, demon-possessed men into a herd of pigs. The animals ran screaming into a lake, where they drowned.

✣ DOGS
'As a dog returns to its vomit, so a fool repeats his folly' runs Proverb 26:11. Dogs get quite a few mentions in the Bible but are generally portrayed in a poor light. They licked up the blood of wronged vineyard owner Naboth after he was ordered to be killed by Ahab and Jezebel. And when they too were killed, dogs once again feasted on their grisly remains.

✣ BEARS
A gang of youths jeered the prophet Elisha: 'Go on up, you

baldhead!' He cursed them and two bears came out of the woods to maul the youths, killing forty-two of them. A kind of Old Testament ASBO.

✟ UNICORNS

There are several mentions of unicorns in the King James Version of the Bible, although always in a metaphorical or symbolic sense. It was translated from the Hebrew *re'em*, although more modern translations would interpret this to mean wild ox.

✟ LIONS

Daniel, protected by an angel, survived a night sealed in a den of hungry lions. Old Testament macho men Samson and David both fought and killed lions. Samson returned to the scene of his fight and ate honey from the carcass of the dead beast, then baffled the Philistines by making his gory feast the answer to a confusing riddle.

✟ WHALE

Jonah was swallowed by a whale – or, at least, a 'great fish' – on his eventful trip to warn the evil city of Nineveh of its forthcoming destruction. It carried him alive for three days and three nights.

✟ BEHEMOTH

Mystery surrounds the identity of the animal which God, in the book of Job, calls 'the behemoth'. The Hebrew word means 'gigantic beast'. It has great strength and power: 'his tail sways like a cedar; the sinews of his thighs are close knit. His bones are tubes of bronze, his limbs like rods of iron. He ranks first among the works of God.' Some believe it to be a hippopotamus, rhinoceros or elephant. Some extreme Creationists believe the behemoth to be a dinosaur – the idea that humans and dinosaurs lived alongside each other supports their theory that the earth is only a few thousand years old.

SHOPPING FOR JESUS

Christian merchandise is big business, especially in the USA, where the majority of the following items are produced.

ARMOR OF GOD PJS

Inspired by Ephesians 6:10, these silky white pyjamas in three sizes come with shield-shaped pillow and helmet and have a crusading look – white with a bold red cross, bearing the legends Faith, Truth, Salvation and Righteousness.

'With their belief in Jesus and his protection children will feel safe and secure during the night as they sleep' (www.armorofgodpjs.com).

SCRIPTURE CANDY

A wide range of sweets, from chocolate and gum to mint sticks and jelly beans, each of which carries an inspirational Bible verse on the wrapper.

'Since we give out candy as "treats" during the holiday, if we could wrap the Word around the candy, every piece we gave out would have the possibility of planting a seed in a person's life' (www.scripturecandy.com).

GOSPEL GOLF BALLS

As the name suggests, these golf balls are inscribed with various good news verses from the Bible.

'If you're playing great, good. If you're spraying the ball, well ... lose a golf ball, share the Gospel' (Revelation Products, USA).

VIRTUE PERFUME

The 'world's first spiritual perfume' blends biblical fragrances such as apricot, fig and pomegranate, and offers the following directions for use: 'Begin your spiritual practice (prayer, meditation, contemplation, etc.); establish your desired spiritual state; smell your wrist, maintaining awareness of your spiritual state; keep repeating this association; in the course of your day, let it remind you of your spiritual state by smelling your wrist' (www.virtueperfume.com).

✤

HOLY FOLKS

Each of these four Cabbage-Patch-style cuddly Bible toys has praying hands and carries a unique accessory – Jesus has a shepherd's crook, Mary a baby Jesus, Moses two stone tablets and Noah a pair of baby elephants. 'Always faithful! Always smiling! Your pray and play pals!' (www.holyfolks.com).

✤

HOLY SOCKS

This attractive range of socks gives you faith on your feet; cartoons illustrate various Bible tales and every set comes with its own original story, poem or meditation. 'Makes people think and points to the faith walk and the spiritual journey we are all on, whether we realise it or not' (www.holysocks.co.uk).

✤

CHRISTIAN SOAP

Mustard seeds, frankincense and myrrh are just some
of the scriptural ingredients of these products, delivered
gift-wrapped with a special Bible verse.
'Hand-made soaps, lotions, balms and body washes
created for the Christian community. Pamper the only
body God gave you. Check out our new line of pure Dead
Sea Mud and Bath Salts for exfoliation and drawing out
impurities of the skin' (www.edensbotanicals.com).

✢

BIBLEMAN

The 'widely acclaimed' DVD adventures of the purple and
yellow masked crusader who fights injustice with the Word
of God, also has action figure, costume, video game and
Bibleman Biblezine spin-off products.
'Bibleman uses the two-edged sword of scripture to cut to
the heart of young Zach's problem with disrespect—only to
be nicked by the other edge of that sword himself! Profes-
sor Snortinskoff is clever, but by relying on God's word,
Bibleman learns the danger of toxic disrespect and defeats
another dastardly scheme' (www.bibleman.com).

✢

THE NANO BIBLE

This astonishing pendant is a small glass crystal coated
with a thin layer of chromium, on which the entire Holy
Bible has been reproduced in microscopic size using nan-
otechnology. Available in three different translations in
yellow gold, white gold or sterling silver.
'If God is in all things, and if Christians hold the Holy
Bible to be the Word of God, then what better way to

remember him and honour his Word, than to be able to "wear" it at all times and in all places? Yes, folks! We believe that even in this crazy world, there IS a place for God and his Word in our hectic, impossible daily lives … So don't wait, and make room in your life for the Nano Bible™ starting today!' (www.nano-bible.com).

✟

THE POPE'S COLOGNE

A distinguished cologne 'with notes of violet and citrus' made using the private formula of Pope Pius IX (1792–1878). 'We have followed this complex, exclusive formula meticulously, using the same essential oils that his perfumers used 150 years ago. We believe that we have succeeded in capturing the same fragrance that he and those around him enjoyed so long ago' (www.thepopescologne.com).

'If God did not exist, it would be necessary to invent him.'

FRANÇOIS VOLTAIRE

⁂{ THE PERSECUTED CHURCH }⁂

The World Watch List is an annual list of countries in which Christians face persecution and poor religious freedom, compiled by Open Doors International. The table is compiled by surveying Christians in each country and assigning values to their answers according to the severity of conditions faced. North Korea, where there are close to half a million Christians, tops the 2008 list for the sixth year in a row.

1. North Korea	16. Qatar
2. Saudi Arabia	17. Vietnam
3. Iran	18. Chechnya
4. Maldives	19. Egypt
5. Bhutan	20. Zanzibar Islands
6. Yemen	21. Iraq
7. Afghanistan	22. Azerbaijan
8. Laos	23. Libya
9. Uzbekistan	24. Mauritania
10. China	25. Burma
11. Eritrea	26. Sudan
12. Somalia	27. Oman
13. Turkmenistan	28. Cuba
14. Comoros	29. Brunei
15. Pakistan	30. India

⁎⟩ DISPUTING THE CANON ⟨⁎

The deuterocanonicals are certain books of the Bible which have not been universally accepted by Christians as canon, or inspired by God. The 1566 Council of Trent formalised seven books as canon, and these have since remained an official part of the Bible recognised by Roman Catholics and Orthodox Christians. But these seven, and a few bits from some of the other books, were rejected by 16th-century reformers and most Bibles in the Protestant tradition either disregard them completely or include them in a separate section called 'The Apocrypha'.

Some Christians, therefore, are familiar with a seventy-three-book Bible while others would be bemused to discover a copy of their Holy Book with titles such as '1 Maccabees' or 'Bel and the Dragon' listed on the contents page. It is for the latter group that a brief summary of the deuterocanonicals is given here.

TOBIT

Demonstrating God's faithfulness to those that are faithful to him, Tobit tells the story of the poor, blind but pious, titular Jew's son, Tobias, and his journey with the angel Raphael which led to Tobit clearing his debts and regaining his sight and Tobias rescuing and marrying the beautiful Sarah.

✟

JUDITH

Tells the story of the young widow, Judith, who rescues the besieged Jewish city of Bethulia from the Assyrian army by seducing and beheading the general Holofernes.

✟

1 AND 2 MACCABEES

These two books are primarily histories, recounting the revolt against the Greek Seleucid Empire's occupation of Judea, the hero of which was the warrior Judas Maccabeus.

✣

WISDOM

This philosophical meditation on righteousness and divine wisdom was influential on many of the New Testament writers. It was traditionally believed to have been written by Solomon, but scholarly evidence now suggests an anonymous author.

✣

ECCLESIASTICUS

Also known as Sirach, this book of proverbs was written by Jesus, Son of Sirach, known as Ben-Sira.

✣

BARUCH

A devotional text written by Baruch, a
disciple of the prophet Jeremiah, for the Jewish
captives in Babylon in the 6th century BC.

✛

THE LETTER OF JEREMIAH

This book is included in Catholic Bibles as chapter 6 of
Baruch, although the authorship is different. It warns Jews
against adopting Babylonian idol-worshipping practices.

✛

*The following three texts are included within the book of Daniel in
Roman Catholic and Orthodox Bibles:*

THE PRAYER OF AZARIAH

Tells of the three youths – Shadrach, Meshach and Abed-
nego – who survived King Nebuchadnezzar's fiery furnace.

✛

SUSANNA

A morality tale in which two elderly voyeurs spy on the
bathing Susanna, before being brought to task by Daniel.

✛

BEL AND THE DRAGON

A chapter of the book of Daniel in which he slays the
Babylonians' dragon-god and sits in the lions' den.

✛

ADDITIONS TO ESTHER

The deuterocanonical Bibles also include six extra chapters
in the book of Esther – prayer-heavy texts that some feel
were written to give the book a more religious tone.

✤

Other variations on the biblical canon:

- The Greek and Slavonic Orthodox churches include 1 Esdras,
  3 Maccabees, the Prayer of Manasseh and Psalm 151.
- The Georgian Orthodox Church includes 4 Maccabees and
  2 Esdras.
- The Ethiopian Orthodox Church includes the Apocalypse of
  Ezra, Jubilees, Enoch, 1–3 Meqabyan and 4 Baruch.
- The Syriac Peshitta Bible includes Psalms 152–5, 2 Baruch and
  the Letter of Baruch.

'To err is human; to forgive, divine.'

ALEXANDER POPE

✳⟨ CHURCHES AND CATHEDRALS ⟩✳

THE OLDEST, **LARGEST**, *smallest*, TALLEST

THE OLDEST

The oldest Christian church in the UK was built around 320 in Colchester, Essex, and the ruins can still be seen in the town.

The oldest church still in use in England is St Martin's, Canterbury. Its exact date of origin is unclear but we know that its use as a place of worship dates back to at least 560, and the building still contains signs of both Roman and Saxon architecture. When Augustine arrived in Canterbury in 597, Queen Bertha, the Christian wife of the pagan King Ethelbert, was already worshipping at the church. Dedicated to St Martin of Tours.

The oldest church in Wales is thought to be Llanrhychwyn Church above the Conwy Valley in North Wales. Although the current church building dates back to the 11th century, it stands on the site of the church built by Rhychwyn, the son of Prince Helig ap Glannog, about 500 years earlier.

The oldest surviving Christian building in the UK is a monk's cell on the isle of Eileachan Naoimh, Strathclyde, built by St Brendan around 542.

World's oldest
The Church of the Holy Sepulchre, built on the site of
Jesus' crucifixion in Jerusalem, and the Church of the
Nativity, built on the site of his birth in Bethlehem, both
date to around 330. In 2005, archaeologists uncovered the
remains of what is probably an even older church in
Megiddo, Israel, formerly the ancient city of Armageddon.

The oldest wooden church in Britain
St Andrew's, in Greenstead, Essex, whose nave
is still built from the trunks of enormous oak
trees dating back to the 11th century (carbon dating
suggests that some of the wood dates to 850).

The oldest church door in Britain
St Botolph's, in Hadstock, Essex. Around 1020, a Dane
was flayed alive in Hadstock for committing sacrilege, and
his skin nailed to the church door. A piece of his skin was
discovered underneath one of the hinges and is kept on
display in the museum of nearby Saffron Walden.

The oldest church tower clock in Britain
The oldest working tower clock can be found on St Mary's,
in Rye, Sussex. It was made by Lewys Billiard of Winchelsea
in 1560, although it is now powered electrically.

Two towers
St Andrew's, in Rugby, Warwickshire, is the only church in the world
to have two towers, each with a complete ring of working bells. One
was built in the 14th century, the other in the 19th century.

The oldest church wind vane in Britain
The church of The Assumption of St Mary and St Nicholas,
in Etchingham, Sussex, carries the oldest wind vane. Dated
to around 1370, it is made of copper in the shape of an
inverted banner in the arms of Sir William of Enchyngham,
who rebuilt the church in the late 14th century.

THE **LARGEST**

The minster church of St John the Evangelist, in Beverley,
Yorkshire, which covers 29,840 square feet, is the largest
in Britain. It is also curious for housing the world's largest
collection of carvings of medieval musical instruments,
and the largest combined area of stained glass windows in
the UK (totalling 25,000 square feet)! The largest church
in Britain that is not a minster is Holy Trinity and Holy
Apostles, in Hull, Yorkshire, at 27,235 square feet.

The largest cathedral in Britain is Liverpool Cathedral,
at 104,275 square feet.

World's largest
The Basilica of Our Lady of Peace of Yamoussoukro,
Ivory Coast (approximately 322,900 square feet, capacity
18,000 people, completed 1989 having taken four years
to build), beating St Peter's Basilica in Vatican City
(approximately 247,600 square feet, capacity 60,000
people, completed 1615 having taken 109 years to build).
The incredible Basilica of Our Lady was built at the behest
of Ivorian president Felix Houphouet-Boigny when he
decided Yamoussoukro, his place of birth, would become

the country's new capital. The building was consecrated by
Pope John Paul II, but only after the Vatican had decreed
that it must not be higher than St Peter's. Accordingly, the
mighty building's dome is just slightly lower than that of its
rival ... although the cross on top of it is 55 feet higher! It
also has the world's largest combined area of stained glass
windows (totalling 80,000 square feet).

The largest cathedral in the world is St John the Divine, Cathedral of New York, which covers 121,000 square feet.

Largest stained glass window
Gloucester Cathedral, whose east window is 2736 square feet.

World's largest stained glass window
The Resurrection Mausoleum in Justice, Illinois, whose main window is 22,381 square feet.

THE *smallest*

Bremilham Church, in the grounds of a farm in Foxley-cum-Bremliham, Wiltshire, is Britain's smallest church building, measuring only 11 feet by 10 feet, and holds just one service a year. It has a single pew and can seat four people, with standing room for six more. The smallest church in regular use is Culbone Church, in Porlock Weir, Somerset, which measures 35 feet by 12 feet. It seats about thirty people, not particularly comfortably.

The UK's smallest cathedral is the 2142 square foot Cumbrae Cathedral (the cathedral of the diocese of the Isles) at Millport, Cumbrae Isle, Strathclyde.

World's smallest
Cross Island Chapel, Oneida, NY, USA (4 feet by 7 feet). And the world's smallest cathedral is Christ Catholic Church in Highlandville, Missouri, USA, which is 14 feet by 17 feet and seats eighteen people.

THE TALLEST

St Walburge's, in Preston, Lancashire, has a spire 309 feet tall, making it the tallest church in Britain. It is also taller than most cathedrals, with only four – Salisbury, St Paul's, Liverpool and Norwich – standing higher. It was built in 1853 and the base of the tower is made from limestone sleepers from the local railway.

World's tallest

The Chicago Temple of the First Methodist Church in Chicago, Illinois, has the tallest spire at 568 feet above street level. Ulm Münster, in Germany, has the tallest cathedral spire (530 feet)

✢⟨ THE POPES ⟩✢

A complete list of the names of Popes of the Roman Catholic Church (as listed in the Annuario Pontificio*), arranged in order of the number of men who have shared the same name.*

1
Agatho
Anacletus
Anicetus
Anterus
Caius
Conon
Constantine
Cornelius
Dionysius
Donus
Eleutherius
Eusebius
Eutychian
Evaristus
Fabian
Formosus
Hilarius
Hormisdas
Hyginus
Lando
Liberius
Linus
Marcellinus
Mark
Miltiades
Peter
Pontian

Romanus
Sabinian
Severinus
Silverius
Simplicius
Siricius
Sisinnius
Soter
Symmachus
Telesphorus
Valentine
Vigilius
Vitalian
Zachary
Zephyrinus
Zosimus

2
Adeodatus
Agapetus
Damasus
Gelasius
John Paul
Marcellus
Marinus
Paschal
Pelagius
Theodore

3
Callixtus
Felix[§]
Julius
Lucius
Martin*
Sylvester
Victor

4
Anastasius
Eugene
Honorius
Sergius

5
Celestine
Nicholas
Sixtus

6
Adrian
Paul

7
Alexander[§]

8
Boniface[§]
Urban

9
Stephen[†]

12
Pius

13
Innocent
Leo

14
Clement

15
Benedict[§]

16
Gregory

21
John[‡][§]

* Although the last Martin was Pope Martin V, Popes Martin II and Martin III were actually known as Marinus I and Marinus II respectively.

† Discounting pope-elect Stephen (AD 752) who died between election and ordination.

‡ There was never a Pope John XX

§ Discounts the antipopes (people who have made a claim to be lawful Pope in opposition to the officially recognised Pope) of this name even though they have regnal numbering

✳ POPE FACTS ✳

LONGEST REIGN
Pius IX, at 31 years and 236 days (1846–78).

✜

SHORTEST REIGN
Stephen II, at two days (752).

✜

LONGEST LIVED
St Angelo, who died in 681 at the age of 106. The preceding
fact may not be true – we have no way of checking; if that's
the case then the next eldest is Leo XIII, who we can
reliably believe died in 1903, aged 93 years old.

✜

YOUNGEST ELECTED POPE
John XII, at 18 years old (in 955).

✜

BRITISH POPE
The only British Pope was Adrian IV (real name
Nicholas Brakespear) in 1154.

✜

❊⟨ Christians from Classic Literature ⟩❊

THE PILGRIMS
The Canterbury Tales (1387–1400) by Geoffrey Chaucer

SIR OLIVER MARTEXT
As You Like It (1599) by William Shakespeare

CHRISTIAN
The Pilgrim's Progress (1678) by John Bunyan

ABRAHAM ADAMS
Joseph Andrews (1742) by Henry Fielding

DR PRIMROSE
The Vicar of Wakefield (1766) by Oliver Goldsmith

MR WILLIAM COLLINS
Pride and Prejudice (1813) by Jane Austen

BOB CRATCHIT
A Christmas Carol (1843) by Charles Dickens

THE REV. OBADIAH SLOPE
Barchester Towers (1857) by Anthony Trollope

FATHER BROWN
Fifty-two short stories (1911–36) by G. K. Chesterton

THE PATIENT
The Screwtape Letters (1942) by C. S. Lewis

✢⟨ THE TEN COMMANDMENTS ⟩✢

Three months into their flight from the tyrannies of Egypt the Israelites camped in the desert at the foot of Mount Sinai, the most southernmost point on their journey to the Promised Land. God called Moses to the top of the mountain and revealed the following ten laws for his people.

ONE GOD
You shall have no other gods before me.

✤

NO IDOLS
You shall not make for yourself an idol in the form of anything in heaven above or on the earth beneath or in the waters below.

✤

DON'T BLASPHEME
You shall not misuse the name of the Lord your God.

✤

OBSERVE SABBATH
Remember the Sabbath day by keeping it holy. Six days you shall labour and do all your work, but the seventh day is a Sabbath to the Lord your God.

✤

HONOUR PARENTS
Honour your mother and father, so that you may live long in the land the Lord your God is giving you.

✤

DON'T KILL
You shall not commit murder.

✦

DON'T COMMIT ADULTERY
You shall not commit adultery.

✦

DON'T STEAL
You shall not steal.

✦

DON'T LIE
You shall not give false testimony against your neighbour.

✦

DON'T COVET
You shall not covet your neighbour's house. You shall
not covet your neighbour's wife, or his manservant
or maidservant, his ox or donkey, or anything that
belongs to your neighbour.

✦

✻⟨ ten 21st-century commandments ⟩✻

Connoisseurs of Christian curiosities may enjoy browsing the Old Testament for oddball laws that we assume no longer apply to us today. 'Do not cut the hair at the sides of your head or clip off the edges of your beard,' commands the Lord in Leviticus 19:27. And 'if two men are fighting and the wife of one of them comes to rescue her husband from his assailant, and she reaches out and seizes him by his private parts, you shall cut off her hand. Show her no pity,' instructs Deuteronomy 25:11–12.

But the truly curious lies closer to home. The following ten laws are still unrepealed today.

It is illegal to wear a fake moustache that
causes laughter in church.

Alabama, United States

Shotguns are required to be taken to church in the event of a
Native American attack.

Maine and South Carolina, United States

If a child burps during church, his parent may be arrested.

Nebraska, United States

A person may not walk around on Sundays with an ice
cream cone in his/her pocket.

New York, United States

Ministers are forbidden from performing marriages when
either the bride or groom is drunk.

Pennsylvania, United States

No Christian parent may require their children to pick up
trash from the highway on Easter day.

Tennessee, United States

It is illegal to deny the existence of God.

Vermont, United States

Horses of more than one year old are forbidden
in a place of worship.

Virginia, United States

No member of the clergy may tell a joke from the pulpit.

West Virginia, United States

Eating mince pies on Christmas Day is banned.

United Kingdom

⸻ THE ROAD TO CANTERBURY *⸻*

*This list shows the number of times an Archbishop of Canterbury
has been appointed from a church post within each of the current
spread of dioceses in the Church of England and Church in Wales.*

18 London

16 Canterbury

11 York

9 Winchester

8 Bath and Wells

6 Lincoln

5 Chichester

4 Worcester

3 Ely, Oxford

2 Norwich, Rochester

1 Bangor, Chester, Exeter, Hereford,
Leicester, Lichfield/Coventry, Monmouth,
St Albans, St David's, Truro

0 Birmingham, Blackburn, Bradford,
Bristol, Carlisle, Chelmsford, Derby,
Durham, Gibraltar in Europe, Gloucester,
Guildford, Liverpool, Llandaff, Manchester, Newcastle,
Peterborough, Portsmouth, Ripon and Leeds, St Asaph,
St Edmundsbury and Ipswich, Salisbury, Sheffield, Sodor
and Man, Southwark, Southwell, Swansea and Brecon, Wakefield

The current Archbishop of Canterbury, Dr Rowan Williams, is the
first man since the Reformation to be appointed from a position
outside the Church of England (he was previously Bishop of Monmouth and Archbishop of Wales in the Church in Wales).

There have been thirty-four Archbishops since the Reformation. Prior to that, several Archbishops were appointed from positions in the Roman Catholic Church outside England or Wales – six from jobs in Rome, and three from jobs in France. Five Archbishops were either appointed from secular positions or the records are unclear what they were doing before being appointed to the see.

'A man can no more diminish God's glory by refusing to worship him than a lunatic can put out the sun by scribbling the word "darkness" on the walls of his cell.'

C. S. Lewis

⁂{ DEADLY SINS AND HOLY VIRTUES }⁂

Warning against the seven deadly vices has been a fundamental aspect of Christian teaching dating back to the Middle Ages. The vices, listed here in traditional order of seriousness, were commonly linked to a corresponding virtue.

VICES	VIRTUES
Lust	Chastity
Gluttony	Temperance
Greed	Charity
Sloth	Diligence
Wrath	Patience
Envy	Kindness
Pride	Humility

In March 2008, the Vatican suggested seven new mortal sins for the modern age:

- Abortion
- Paedophilia
- Ruining the environment
- Conducting morally debatable scientific experiments
- Allowing genetic manipulations which alter DNA or compromise embryos
- Taking or dealing in drugs
- Social injustice causing poverty or the excessive accumulation of wealth by a few

❧ A TABLE OF KINDRED AND AFFINITY ❧

Wherein whosoever are related are forbidden by the Church of England to marry together (as printed for curious eyes at the back of the 1662 Book of Common Prayer)

A man may not marry his	*A woman may not marry her*
mother	father
daughter	son
adopted daughter	adopted son
father's mother	father's father
mother's mother	mother's father
son's daughter	son's son
daughter's daughter	daughter's son
sister	brother
wife's mother	husband's father
wife's daughter	husband's son
father's wife	mother's husband
son's wife	daughter's husband
father's father's wife	father's mother's husband
mother's father's wife	mother's mother's husband
wife's father's mother	husband's father's father
wife's mother's mother	husband's mother's father
wife's daughter's daughter	husband's son's son
wife's son's daughter	husband's daughter's son
son's son's wife	son's daughter's husband
daughter's son's wife	daughter's daughter's husband
father's sister	father's brother
mother's sister	mother's brother
brother's daughter	brother's son
sister's daughter	sister's son

In this table the term 'brother' includes a brother of the half-blood, and the term 'sister' includes a sister of the half-blood.

❋⟨ THE EXORCIST'S TOOLS ⟩❋

According to the Roman Catholic Church's official Rite of Exorcism, dating from the Second Vatican Council of 1964 and slightly revised in 1999, the following items are required for the exorcism of a demon from a possessed person. Only authorised priests may perform this ceremony, and they should first go to confession and Mass and implore God's help in fervent prayer.

A BIBLE

Several readings from the Psalms and the Gospels may be required, and some also believe that demons are terrified of and will shy away from the physical form of the Bible itself.

✜

A WOODEN CRUCIFIX

Also a sign of power and defence over demons. The priest is also required to make the sign of the cross on a number of occasions in the ceremony, over himself, any other people present and the possessed – at various times on his/her brow, breast and lips.

✜

HOLY WATER

This is normal tap water with a small sprinkling of blessed salt, the whole mixture then exorcised and blessed by a priest.

✜

ANOINTING OIL

As used by the Israelites in the anointing of kings and consecration of certain people. The oil should be pure, virgin olive oil, although it is occasionally scented with balsam, making it *chrism*.

✜

OFFICIAL VESTMENTS
The priest should wear a surplice (normally white) and a purple stole, the end of which is at one point placed on the neck of the possessed.

✜

RELICS OF THE SAINTS
Although not mentioned in the official rite, some specialists believe any relic of a saint will also aid the process of exorcism if touched to the head or body of the possessed.

'God and the doctor we alike adore
But only when in danger, not before;
The danger o'er, both are alike requited,
God is forgotten, and the doctor slighted.'

JOHN OWEN

*'God writes the gospel not in the Bible
alone, but on trees, and flowers,
and clouds, and stars.'*

Martin Luther

∗⟨ Jesus' Family Tree ⟩∗

*The genealogy presented on the following pages is that written by
Luke, although it is at odds with that of Matthew, which traces a
different line of descent from Jesus back to David. In Matthew's
genealogy, Joseph's father is given as Jacob and leads back to David
through the line of Solomon rather than his older brother Nathan.*

It could be that while Matthew intended to demonstrate Jesus'
legal claim to the throne of Israel as a direct heir, Luke was more
interested in showing Jesus' blood link to David through his natural mother Mary (Joseph not being his natural father). It has
been suggested that even though Luke says Heli was Joseph's
father, he was actually Mary's father.

45

CREATION
C. 2500BC

FLOOD

C. 2000BC

C. 1000BC

God

Adam ·············· *Created by God, in his likeness, on the sixth*

Seth ············· *day of Creation.*

Enosh

Kenan ······ *Adam and Eve's third son, born after one of his*

brothers, Abel, was killed by the other, Cain.

Mahalalel

Jared

Enoch

Methuselah ····· *The oldest man listed in the Bible.*

Lamech

Noah ················· *A righteous man, blameless among the people*

Shem *of his time. Noah and his sons, Shem, Ham*

Arphaxad ······ *and Japheth, were chosen to survive the Flood.*

Cainan *God then established a new covenant with*

Shelah *Noah and all his descendants.*

Eber

Peleg

Reu ······ *Born two years after the Flood.*

Serug

Nahor

Terah *Established an everlasting covenant with God,*

Abraham ············· *making him 'father of many nations'.*

Isaac ····················· *Son of Abraham and Sarah.*

Jacob ···················· *Son of Isaac and Rebekah, and father of the*

Judah ·············· *Twelve Tribes of Israel. Bought the birthright*

Perez *and Abrahamic blessing from his elder brother*

Hezron *Esau, for a bowl of soup.*

Ram

Amminadab

Nahshon ······ *Fourth son of Jacob and Leah, and founder*

Salmon *of the Tribe of Judah.*

Boaz ························ *His marriage to Obed's mother Ruth is told in*

Obed *the book of Ruth.*

Jesse ······················ *'A shoot will come up from the stump of Jesse;*

David ·············· *from his roots a Branch will bear fruit'*

Nathan *(Isaiah 11:1).*

Mattatha

Menna ······ *The first King of Israel in the line, and probably the most*

Melea *celebrated. David had at least eight wives, but it was*

through Bathsheba that Nathan and Solomon were born.

Eliakim
Jonam
Joseph
Judah
Simeon
Levi
Matthat
Jorim
Eliezer
Joshua
Er
Elmadam
Cosam
Addi
Melki
Neri
Shealtiel

C. 500BC

Zerubbabel ·················· *Led the first Jews back to Israel after Babylon-*
Rhesa   *ian captivity in 537 BC. He laid the foundation*
Joanan   *of the Second Temple.*
Joda
Josech
Semein
Mattathias
Maath
Naggai
Esli
Nahum
Amos
Mattathias
Joseph
Jannai
Melki
Levi
Matthat
Heli

C. 5BC

Joseph
Jesus ····························· *Son of God and King of the Jews.*

✣{ THE TWELVE }✣

The apostles are the spiritual forefathers of all Christians. Faithful followers and companions of Jesus during his time on earth, and crusading founders of the early church following his ascension, the Twelve have been venerated throughout Christian history. The legends that surround them are as numerous as the facts, and equally fascinating.

ANDREW

This fisherman, born at Bethsaida, Galilee, was a disciple of John the Baptist when he first encountered Jesus and was called to become the first apostle. He introduced Jesus to his brother Simon (with whom he shared a house in Capernaum), who also became an apostle.

✤ *Feast day*: 30 November

✤ *Patron saint of*: Scotland, Plymouth, fishermen, sufferers of gout and sore throats, old maids, spinsters

✤ *Legend*: Women wishing to find their future husbands have a number of options on and around St Andrew's Day. Sleep naked on the night before, and you will picture the lucky man in your dreams. On the day itself, listen for the sound of barking dogs – he will come from that direction. And, on the day after, seek out and join a group of young people floating cups in a tub – if your cup and that of a young man drift together and are intercepted by a cup marked 'priest', then you are destined to marry him (the young man, not the priest).

BARTHOLOMEW

A good friend of Philip, Bartholomew is mentioned only in the Gospels of Matthew, Mark and Luke, but is commonly believed to be the same man as the apostle named Nathanael in the Gospel of

48

John. Jesus said of Nathanael: 'Here is a true Israelite, in whom there is nothing false.'

✤ *Feast day*: 24 August

✤ *Patron saint of*: Armenia, butchers, bookbinders, cobblers, twitchers and sufferers of nervous diseases, Florentine cheese merchants

✤ *Legend*: The Massacre of St Bartholomew's Eve saw between 10,000 and 100,000 Protestant Huguenots murdered in a series of riots in Paris and across France, starting on the apostle's feast day in 1572, believed to have been instigated by King Charles IX's mother, Catherine de Medici.

JAMES (SON OF ZEBEDEE)

Otherwise known as 'James the Great' to distinguish him from the other apostle of the same name, James and his younger brother John were nicknamed Boanerges – 'Sons of Thunder' – by Jesus. The pair and Simon Peter are considered to be a privileged trio among the apostles, having been selected by Jesus to witness both the Transfiguration and the Agony of Gethsemane – his prayer of pleading the night before he died.

✤ *Feast day*: 25 July

✤ *Patron saint of*: Spain, Chile, conquistadors, sufferers of rheumatism and arthritis, blacksmiths, vets, pilgrims

✤ *Legend*: Nowhere is the legend of James greater than in Spain. It was once (wrongly) believed that he preached in Spain and, according to legend, angels took his body back there after his death (see 'Deaths of the Apostles'). The relics of James are kept at Compostela, destination of one of the world's most famous pilgrimages and founding town of the famous order of the Knights of Santiago.

JAMES (SON OF ALPHAEUS)

Or 'James the Less', probably for no reason other than becoming an apostle after James the Great. brother of Jude.

✧ *Feast day*: 3 May

✧ *Patron saint of*: Uruguay, milliners, pharmacists, dying people

✧ *Legend*: James is said to have spent so much time in prayer that his knees thickened to the size of a camel's.

JOHN

Younger of the 'Sons of Thunder' brothers, believed by many to be the author of the Gospel of John and 'the disciple whom Jesus loved', this former fisherman claimed to be the first person to believe Jesus had risen from the dead, when he and Simon Peter discovered the empty burial cloth in Jesus' tomb.

✧ *Feast day*: 27 December

✧ *Patron saint of*: Asia Minor, authors, publishers, theologians, painters, art dealers, sufferers of burns and poisoning

✧ *Legend*: There are many dramatic stories of John's crusades against paganism and idolatry. When followers of the goddess Artemis stoned him, the rocks turned in mid-air and hit his attackers. On another occasion, fire from heaven killed 200 worshippers of Artemis in response to John's prayers, but he raised them all from the dead.

JUDAS

The only apostle not from the region of Galilee, Judas was born in the city of Kerioth in Judah, hence the surname Iscariot. He was given responsibility for the apostles' money bag, although it was said he helped himself to some of the funds. Infamously, he betrayed Jesus to the Jewish authorities.

✤ *Legend*: Unsurprisingly, Judas has no feast days or causes for his patronage in the historic vista of orthodox Christianity. The closest he received to a sympathetic hearing was veneration by the Gnostic Cainite sect, one of whose texts was the Gospel of Judas which held that his actions were in fact an act of obedience to Jesus, as they fulfilled his prediction of his betrayal and were the catalyst for the events that led to his death, our atonement and the final victory.

JUDE

Also known as Thaddeus, Jude and his brother James are believed to have been cousins of Jesus. Jude was author of the biblical epistle warning against false teachers who were misrepresenting the concept of God's grace.

✤ *Feast day*: 28 October

✤ *Patron saint of*: Florida, hospitals, desperate situations and lost causes

✤ *Legend*: Jude is probably the saint of lost causes because his epistle encourages us to persevere in the faith, although some claim it stems from confusion among early Christians – not understanding the difference between Jude and Judas, they never prayed for the former's help and so devotion to him became a lost cause!

MATTHEW

Matthew was the name taken by tax-collector Levi after he was called by Jesus from his toll booth in Capernaum (the booth probably sat on the road between Damascus and the Mediterranean coast). He went on to host a dinner for Jesus, the apostles and other tax-collectors, to the outrage of local Pharisees. Matthew wrote the Gospel which appears first in the New Testament.

✤ *Feast day*: 21 September

✤ *Patron saint of*: Tax-collectors, accountants, customs officers, security forces, stockbrokers

✤ *Legend*: After the resurrection of Jesus, Matthew is believed to have undertaken a ministry of preaching to other Jews. His travels may have taken him to Ethiopia, where he was martyred.

MATTHIAS

The thirteenth apostle. In the days following Jesus' ascent to heaven, the apostles decided to elect a new member to their number to replace Judas, who had committed suicide. Matthias, who had witnessed all of Jesus' ministry, from his baptism to the ascension, and a man called Barsabbas were shortlisted, and Matthias was chosen after the apostles prayed and drew lots.

✤ *Feast day*: 14 May

✤ *Patron saint of*: Carpenters, tailors, sufferers of smallpox, alcoholics

✤ *Legend*: Records of the early Christian writers such as Origen and Eusebius suggest there was a Gospel of Matthias, although the text is now lost. Among the small extracts to survive is an exhortation to set no value upon the flesh, but rather to increase the growth of our souls through faith and knowledge.

PHILIP

Philip from Bethsaida was called personally by Jesus to join the apostles, and persuaded his friend Nathanael to come and meet the Messiah also. It was Philip who, on behalf of the apostles, asked Jesus to 'show us the Father' to help them believe, to which Jesus replied that anyone who had seen him had seen the Father.

✢ *Feast day*: 3 May

✢ *Patron saint of*: Luxembourg, pastry chefs

✢ *Legend*: Philip was unusual among the apostles in that he was already married, with children, when he joined the Twelve. Following the events of the Gospels, he is believed to have preached across Greece and Asia, meeting his end in Hierapolis (in modern-day Turkey) after angering the proconsul of the city by converting his wife.

SIMON PETER

Upon being introduced by his brother Andrew, fisherman Simon was given the name Cephas (translated as Peter, meaning 'rock') by Jesus. He is always named first in lists of the apostles, and in the accounts of the Bible he seemed to act as leader of the group. Jesus later told Simon Peter that he was the rock on which he would build his Church, and also that he would give him the keys of the kingdom of heaven. Peter was recognised in the early church as 'Prince of the Apostles' and, in establishing the see of Rome, became the first in the line of Popes that continues to this day.

✢ *Feast day*: 29 June

✢ *Patron saint of*: Rome, bridge-builders, shoemakers, watch-makers, stonemasons, fishermen, sufferers of feet problems, Popes, the Universal Church

✤ *Legend*: The legend of Simon Peter is immense and surely
the magnitude of his rise from humble beginnings to historic
legacy is bettered only by that of Jesus himself. Spiritual
and ecclesiastical significance aside, he must also be one
of the most recurring characters in jokes and cartoons, as
the bearded, cloud-walking guardian of the pearly gates of
heaven.

SIMON THE ZEALOT

So called for his zeal in practising Jewish law before his call to join
the Twelve, although some believe he had actually been a member
of the sect of Zealots who sought to end Roman oppression of the
Jews through underground, sometimes militant means (it has
been claimed that Judas was also a Zealot).

✤ *Feast day*: 28 October

✤ *Patron saint of*: Curriers, tanners, sawyers

✤ *Legend*: Simon travelled and preached widely, often with Jude,
as the apostles began to spread the gospel in the first years of
the early church. He is even said to have visited Glastonbury
in England, and there are several claims to the location of his
eventual martyrdom (see 'Deaths of the Apostles').

THOMAS

The epithet 'Doubting Thomas', derived from this apostle's
refusal to accept Jesus' resurrection until he had touched his
wounds for himself, is perhaps a little unfair as the Bible actually
records Thomas as a man of courage and faith. 'Let us also go, that
we may die with him,' he encouraged his fellow disciples.

✤ *Feast day*: 3 July

✤ *Patron saint of*: India, Pakistan, architects, blind people, stonemasons, theologians, people in doubt

✣ *Legend*: Thomas took the gospel to India in a hugely successful mission that saw the building of many new churches across a vast geographic area, although it is said he was so reluctant initially to start this particular journey that he had to be taken to India as the slave of a merchant.

'That the universe was formed by a fortuitous concourse of atoms, I will no more believe than that the accidental jumbling of the alphabet would fall into a most ingenious treatise of philosophy.'

Jonathan Swift

⁂{ EAT, DRINK AND BE MERRY }⁂

In the fashion of good soap opera, some of the Bible's most dramatic scenes occur at the climax of a banquet, party or drunken binge. Here are ten of the wildest bashes, and their 'morning after' consequences.

A PARTY FOR ONE

- *Occasion*: Noah, fresh from surviving the Great Flood, planted a vineyard and drank heavily of its wine one day. This is the first of 247 references to wine or strong drink in the Bible (59 per cent of which appear to be in a positive context, 25 per cent neutral and only 16 per cent – including this episode of Noah's – negative).

- *Guests*: After Noah fell asleep in his tent, drunk and naked, he was discovered by his youngest son, Ham. His two other sons, Shem and Japheth, hid their eyes and covered Noah with a blanket.

- *The morning after*: When he woke and discovered what had happened, Noah flew into a mighty rage and cursed Ham's son, Canaan, to live as a slave to his other sons.

SPOILING THE PARTY FOR EVERYONE

- *Occasion*: A great feast to mark the weaning of Abraham's son Isaac, finally born to his previously barren wife Sarah.

- *Guests*: The household of Abraham, including Sarah's Egyptian handmaid Hagar, who had borne Abraham his only other son, Ishmael, about sixteen years earlier.

- *The morning after*: Jealous of the favour he knew his half-brother would receive, Ishmael mocked little Isaac on his big day. The next morning, at Sarah's demand, Abraham sent Ishmael and Hagar packing to the desert, where the boy

became a talented archer but never received his father's
blessed inheritance.

HOLD ON, YOU'RE NOT ...

🍷 *Occasion*: A wedding feast. Jacob had been working for his
Uncle Laban for seven years, after which time he had been
promised the hand of his youngest daughter, Rachel – 'lovely
in form, and beautiful'.

🍷 *Guests*: All the people of Laban's household. Including his
eldest daughter, Leah – who 'had weak eyes'.

🍷 *The morning after*: A true 'morning after' moment. Jacob
awoke in bed and rolled over to greet his new wife, with whom
he had spent the night. To his horror, he lay next to Leah. 'It's
our custom to marry the eldest daughter first,' protested
Laban, who had orchestrated the deceit. 'Work another seven
years for me and I'll give you Rachel as well!'

CLEANED OUT

🍷 *Occasion*: A lavish banquet hosted by the cruel landowner
Nabal, days after snubbing the request of David for food and
drink for his men. David had previously shown kindness to
Nabal's men.

🍷 *Guests*: Nabal and his entourage partied long and drank
heavily. His wife Abigail snuck in late when Nabal was too
drunk to ask where she had been.

🍷 *The morning after*: Abigail came clean. She had raided her husband's stores, stolen some donkeys and personally delivered
200 loaves of bread, two skins of wine, five dressed sheep, five
seahs of roasted grain, 100 raisin cakes and 200 fig cakes to
David. Nabal had a heart attack, and died.

IT'S NOT WHAT YOU THINK!

- 🎶 *Occasion*: A private dinner party hosted by Esther, Jewish queen of the Persian king Xerxes. As the dinner took place, Xerxes' highest-ranking noble, the anti-Semitic Haman, was plotting to murder Esther's uncle, Mordecai.

- 🎶 *Guests*: Esther, Xerxes and Haman. As was the custom, dinner was taken while reclining on couches.

- 🎶 *The morning after*: After plentiful quantities of Persian wine had been imbibed, Esther exposed Haman's persecution of her people to the king. After Xerxes stormed out of the room, Haman begged Esther to save him, virtually toppling over her on her couch … but Xerxes returned at that moment, discovering his trusty officer apparently molesting his beloved wife. Haman was hanged on the very gallows he had prepared for Mordecai.

A HELLRAISING PARTY

- 🎶 *Occasion*: One of a regular series of soirees held by the rich sons and daughters of Job — blameless and upright, the greatest man of his day among the people of the East.

- 🎶 *Guests*: All seven of Job's sons and all three of his daughters were feasting and drinking at the oldest brother's house. Events were being observed by Satan, who had a wager with God that he could turn Job against him.

- 🎶 *The morning after*: Job, who did not attend his children's parties, received word that during the festivities all his livestock were either stolen by raiders or destroyed by fire from the sky, almost all his servants murdered and, finally, that a mighty wind had collapsed the party house and killed all his sons and daughters. Job tore his robes and shaved his head and undertook a mighty lament against God and the injustice of the universe.

THE WRITING ON THE WALL

- 🎵 *Occasion*: A mighty, hedonistic banquet hosted in the royal palace by Belshazzar, the last King of Babylon.
- 🎵 *Guests*: Belshazzar invited 1,000 of his nobles and they, his wives and his concubines drank wine in gold and silver goblets that the Babylonians had ransacked from the Temple in Jerusalem, and toasted their pagan idols.
- 🎵 *The morning after*: The revelries were dramatically interrupted by the ghostly appearance of the fingers of a human hand, which etched four words predicting the fall of the Babylonian Empire. Belshazzar turned pale and collapsed with fright. The prophecy was fulfilled as he was slain that very night.

A NASTY PIECE OF WORK

- 🎵 *Occasion*: The birthday of King Herod Antipas, Galilee.
- 🎵 *Guests*: High officials, military commanders and anyone who was anyone in Galilee. Herod's new wife, Herodias (also the wife of his still-living half-brother, Herod Philip), and her daughter, Salome, who performed a lascivious dance for the guests.
- 🎵 *The morning after*: So enamoured was he with his stepdaughter's performance that Herod offered her the gift of her choice. She chose the head of rabble-rousing prophet John the Baptist, who had been preaching against the immorality of Herod and her mother; it was delivered to her on a plate.

RSVP

- 🎵 *Occasion*: A delicious wedding banquet, given by a gracious king in honour of his son.
- 🎵 *Guests*: Many important guests were invited, but they refused to come. Some ignored the invitation completely, others

killed the servants who had delivered the message. The king, enraged, sent his armies to kill these murderers and filled his banquet with a new set of guests, gathered from the street corners of society. But one man arrived at the party without the proper wedding clothes, and was thrown outside into the darkness.

The morning after: Such is the kingdom of heaven, Jesus told us. Many are invited, but few are chosen.

THE PRODIGAL

- 🍃 *Occasion*: Not so much one party but a spree of wild living, as a youngest son blew his entire inheritance in a distant land.

- 🍃 *Guests*: Who *wasn't* invited?

- 🍃 *The morning after*: Just as his purse ran dry, a famine hit the land and the son found himself reduced to feeding pigs, enviously eyeing their swill. He returned repentant to his father, who threw a feast to celebrate. So will God celebrate those who were lost but are found again.

'I believe in one God the Father Almighty, Maker of heaven and earth, And of all things visible and invisible: And in one Lord Jesus Christ, the only-begotten Son of God, Begotten of his Father before all worlds, God of God, Light of Light, Very God of very God, Begotten, not made, Being of one substance with the Father, By whom all things were made.'

THE BOOK OF COMMON PRAYER, 1662

✻⟨ MOST POPULAR HYMNS ⟩✻

This top ten of most popular hymns, as selected by tens of thousands of viewers of the British television show Songs of Praise *in a 2005 survey, comprises an intriguing mix of old and new.*

10

SHINE, JESUS, SHINE

This hymn, written in 1987 by Graham Kendrick, was sung at the largest ever open-air mass in Manila in 1995, where Pope John Paul II was seen to be swinging his cane in time to the music.

9

IN CHRIST ALONE

Written in 2002 by British and Irish songwriters Stuart Townend and Keith Getty, this hymn has already been recorded over a hundred times by various contemporary artists.

8

GUIDE ME, O THOU GREAT REDEEMER

This unofficial Welsh national anthem was written in 1745 by William Williams, *Y pêr ganiedydd* (the sweet singer), and translated into English by Peter Williams. It is sung heartily by Welsh rugby crowds and was one of the hymns at the funeral of Diana, Princess of Wales, in 1997.

7

MAKE ME A CHANNEL OF THY PEACE

Based on the prayer 'Lord, Make me an Instrument of thy Peace', traditionally ascribed to St Francis of Assisi, this is often sung on Remembrance Sunday in the United Kingdom and, like 'Guide Me, O thou Great Redeemer', was sung at Diana's funeral.

6

BE STILL, FOR THE PRESENCE OF THE LORD

Written in 1986 by Australian songwriter and evangelist David Evans.

5

LOVE DIVINE, ALL LOVES EXCELLING

This popular wedding hymn was written by Charles Wesley in 1747 and is probably best known to the tune *Blaenwern* by William Rowlands. Its original second verse is often omitted because some (including the author's brother, John Wesley) disapproved of the line 'Take away our bent to sinning', which suggests that we can be completely free of sin in our earthly lives.

4

BE THOU MY VISION

Translated from an Old Irish text believed to have been written in the 8th century by poet Dallan Forgaill. The familiar music is from the Irish folk song 'Slane', which tells of St Patrick defying the pagan king Logaire by lighting candles on Easter Eve and subsequently being allowed to continue his missionary work.

3

THE DAY THOU GAVEST

Written in 1870 by John Ellerton, this hymn, which includes the lines 'Thy throne shall never, Like earth's proud empires, pass away', was a favourite of Queen Victoria and was also played at the ceremony of Britain's handover of Hong Kong to China in 1997.

2

DEAR LORD AND FATHER OF MANKIND

The words of this hymn are actually the last six verses of a poem, *The Brewing of Soma* (1872), by American Quaker John Greenleaf Whittier, which tells the cautionary tale of Hindu Vedic priests going into the woods, brewing themselves a cauldron of hallucinogenic soma and getting stoned.

1

HOW GREAT THOU ART

Translated into English by the missionary Stuart Hine, from the Russian translation of a 19th-century Swedish poem by Carl Gustaf Boberg, this chart-topper reached international fame when it was sung over a hundred times by George Beverley Shea at a Billy Graham revival. It was also a favourite of Elvis Presley.

The *Cyber Hymnal* website reports John Newton's 'Amazing Grace' and Fanny Crosby's 'Blessed Assurance' as the world's most popular hymns, based on its own traffic.

✦❧ STATIONS OF THE CROSS ❧✦

Walking the Stations is a practice that stems from the visits to Jerusalem of the first Christian pilgrims, who would follow a set route from Pilate's house to Calvary and seek to replicate the devotion once they returned home. It involves passing reflectively past a series of fourteen representations – usually, although not exclusively, paintings or carvings – of key scenes from Jesus' final hours. The traditional ordering of the Stations is:

1. Jesus is condemned to death
2. Jesus receives the cross
3. *Jesus falls for the first time*
4. *Jesus sees his mother*
5. Simon of Cyrene helps carry the cross
6. *Veronica wipes Jesus' face with her veil*
7. *Jesus falls for the second time*
8. Jesus meets the women of Jerusalem
9. *Jesus falls for the third time*
10. Jesus is stripped of his garments
11. Jesus is nailed to the cross
12. Jesus dies
13. *Jesus' body is removed from the cross*
14. Jesus is laid in the tomb

As six of the Stations are derived from non-biblical traditions (italicised), the following new sequence was devised, in which each scene is based on an actual Gospel account. Pope John Paul II gave this new set of Stations his approval by celebrating them in 1991.

1. Jesus agonises in the Garden of Gethsemane
2. Jesus is betrayed by Judas and arrested
3. Jesus is condemned by the Sanhedrin
4. Jesus is denied by Peter
5. Jesus is condemned to death by Pilate
6. Jesus is scourged and crowned with thorns
7. Jesus bears his cross
8. Simon of Cyrene helps carry the cross
9. Jesus meets the women of Jerusalem
10. Jesus is crucified
11. Jesus promises paradise to the good thief
12. Jesus speaks to Mary and the disciple from the cross
13. Jesus dies on the cross
14. Jesus is laid in the tomb

⁂ THE BOOK OF WORDS ⁂

The essential facts and figures of the Bible. These statistics are obviously subject to change depending on the translation. I have limited the figures to the traditional King James Version (KJV) and the bestselling modern English translation, the New International Version (NIV).

NUMBER OF WORDS
IN THE BIBLE

773,692 (KJV)
752,702 (NIV)

NUMBER OF VERSES
IN THE BIBLE

31,173 (KJV)
31,086 (NIV)

NUMBER OF CHAPTERS
IN THE BIBLE

1189

LONGEST WORD

Maher-Shalal-Hash-Baz
(Isaiah 8:1)

SECOND-LONGEST WORD

Chu-Shan-Rish-A-Tha-Im
(Judges 3:8)

LONGEST VERSE

Then were the king's scribes called at that time in the third month, that is, the month Sivan, on the three and twentieth day thereof; and it was written according to all that Mordecai commanded unto the Jews, and to the lieutenants, and the deputies and rulers of the provinces which are from India unto Ethiopia, an hundred twenty and seven provinces, unto every province according to the writing thereof, and unto every people after their language, and to the Jews according to their writing, and according to their language. (Esther 8:9 – while this has ninety words in the KJV, it has only seventy in the NIV but remains the longest verse.)

SHORTEST VERSE   'Jesus wept' (John 11:35, KJV)
                                     'He said:' (Job 3:2, NIV)

LONGEST CHAPTER   Psalm 119

SHORTEST CHAPTER   Psalm 117 (which is also the Bible's
                                     middle chapter)

THE SHORTEST NAMES   Ai (Joshua 7:2)
IN THE BIBLE   Ar (Numbers 21:15)
                                     Ed (Joshua 22:34)
                                     Ir (1 Chronicles 7:12)
                                     No (Jeremiah 46:25)
                                     Og (Numbers 21:33)
                                     On (Numbers 16:11)
                                     Pe (Psalm 119:129)
                                     So (2 Kings 17:4)
                                     Ur (Genesis 11:28)
                                     Uz (Genesis 10:23)

VERSES OF NOTE

No verse contains all twenty-six letters of the alphabet, but a small number contain twenty-five. Can you work out which letter is missing from the following verses (all KJV)?

'And Adonijah slew sheep and oxen and fat cattle by the stone of Zoheleth, which is by Enrogel, and called all his brethren the king's sons, and all the men of Judah the king's servants.' (1 Kings 1:9)

'And Jabez called on the God of Israel, saying, "Oh that thou wouldest bless me indeed, and enlarge my coast, and that thine hand might be with me, and that thou wouldest keep me from evil, that it may not grieve me!" And God granted him that which he requested.' (1 Chronicles 4:10)

'And I, even I Artaxerxes the king, do make a decree to all the treasurers which are beyond the river, that whatsoever Ezra the priest, the scribe of the law of the God of heaven, shall require of you, it be done speedily.' (Ezra 7:21)

'In the second year of Darius the king, in the sixth month, in the first day of the month, came the word of the Lord by Haggai the prophet unto Zerubbabel the son of Shealtiel, governer of Judah, and to Joshua the son of Josedech, the high priest, saying,' (Haggai 1:1)

'And profited in the Jews' religion above many my equals in mine own nation, being more exceedingly zealous of the traditions of my fathers.' (Galatians 1:14)

'To lift up the hands in prayer gives God glory, but a man with a pitchfork in his hand, a woman with a slop-pail, give him glory too.'

GERARD MANLEY HOPKINS

✢⟨ CHURCH FATHERS TOP TRUMPS ⟩✢

ST ANTONY THE GREAT
c.251–356

Lived: Mt Pispi, Egypt
Beard: Long, thick, sandy
Claim: The first Christian hermit and monk, and founder of Christian monasticism.
Quote: 'If any of you have any authority over me, only one would have been sufficient to fight me' (on fighting demons in the form of wild beasts).

ST AMBROSE
c.339–97

Lived: Milan, Italy
Beard: Short, rough, mutton-chops
Claim: Influential theologian and reforming church leader. Helped the conversion of St Augustine.
Quote: 'The foolish fear death as the greatest of all evils, the wise desire it as a rest after labours and the end of ills.'

ST ATHANASIUS
c.293–373

Lived: Alexandria, Egypt
Beard: Woolly, white, gnomish
Claim: Champion of the First Council of Nicaea and opponent of Arianism.
Quote: 'He became what we are that he might make us what he is.'

ST AUGUSTINE OF HIPPO
354–430

Lived: Hippo, Algeria
Beard: Long, grey, wizardy
Claim: Made popular the concepts of original sin, and just war.
Quote: 'Love and then what you will, do.'

ST BASIL THE GREAT
c.329–79

Lived: Caesarea, Turkey
Beard: Long, dark, horsey
Claim: His learning, eloquence, compassion and correct living highly influential in establishment of Eastern monasticism.
Quote: 'The Christian should offer his brethren simple and unpretentious hospitality.'

ST BENEDICT OF NURSIA
c.480–c.547

Lived: Monte Cassino, Italy
Beard: Bushy, white, cloven
Claim: Writer of the Rule of Benedict and founder of Benedictine monasticism.
Quote: 'Idleness is the enemy of the soul.'

ST BERNARD OF CLAIRVAUX
1090–1153

Lived: Clairvaux, France
Beard: White, short, stubbly
Claim: Influential preacher and mystic, led growth and reform of the Cistercian monastic order.
Quote: 'Everyone is his own enemy.'

ST CLEMENT OF ALEXANDRIA
c.150–c.211

Lived: Alexandria, Egypt
Beard: Long, white, cloven
Claim: Married faith with reason, Christian doctrine with Greek philosophy.
Quote: 'Christ has turned all our sunsets into dawns.'

ST CLEMENT OF ROME
c.30–c.100

Lived: Rome, Italy
Beard: Medium, white, tidy
Claim: The fourth Pope and writer of an epistle to the Corinthians that was once considered part of Scripture.
Quote: 'It is better for a man to confess his sins than to harden his heart.'

ST CYPRIAN
c.200–58

Lived: Carthage, Tunisia
Beard: Medium, white, cloven
Claim: The first African martyr-bishop.
Quote: 'To him who still remains in this world no repentance is too late.'

ST GREGORY THE GREAT
c.540–604

Lived: Rome, Italy
Beard: Short, white, distinguished
Claim: One of the most influential of all popes, reformer and establisher of the Church's political independence.
Quote: 'They are not Angles, but Angels' (on seeing enslaved English boys).

ST GREGORY OF NYSSA
c.350–c.395

Lived: Nyssa, Turkey
Beard: Long, dark, stringy
Claim: A great thinker, preacher and theologian, later hailed as 'Father of the Fathers' for his defence of the doctrine of the Trinity.
Quote: 'True perfection consists in having but one fear, the loss of God's friendship.'

ST IGNATIUS OF ANTIOCH
c.35–c.110

Lived: Antioch, Turkey
Beard: White, wavy, excitable
Claim: Wrestled with wild beasts en route to being martyred in Rome.
Quote: 'Fire and cross and battling with wild beasts, their clawing and tearing, the breaking of bones and mangling of members, the grinding of my whole body, the wicked torments of the devil – let them assail me, so long as I get to Jesus Christ.'

ST IRENAEUS OF LYONS
c.115–c.202

Lived: Lyons, France
Beard: Cloven, bushy, eccentric
Claim: Helped determine the New Testament canon, in particular the four Gospels.
Quote: 'For the whole Church which is throughout the whole world possesses one and the same faith.'

ST JEROME
c.347–420

Lived: Rome, Italy
Beard: White, ragged, rugged
Claim: Translated the Bible into Latin (the *Vulgate*).
Quote: 'Christians are made, not born.'

ST JOHN CHRYSOSTOM
c.347–407

Lived: Constantinople, Turkey
Beard: Dark, trim, serious
Claim: Known as the 'golden-mouthed' for his passionate biblical preaching.
Quote: 'Faithfulness in little things is a big thing.'

ST DOMINIC
1170–1221

Lived: Toulouse, France
Beard: Brown, soft, fluffy
Claim: Founded the Dominican monastic order, and credited with invention of the rosary.
Quote: 'Zeal must be met by zeal, humility by humility, false sanctity by real sanctity, preaching falsehood by preaching truth.'

ST FRANCIS OF ASSISI
1181–1226

Lived: Assisi, Italy
Beard: Short, rough, wild
Claim: Founded the Franciscan and Poor Clares orders. Blessed with stigmata and a love for animals. Patron saint of zoos.
Quote: 'Sanctify yourself and you will sanctify society.'

ST IGNATIUS OF LOYOLA
1491–1556

Lived: Rome, Italy
Beard: Thin, dark, neat
Claim: Founder of the Jesuits, writer of the *Spiritual Exercises*.
Quote: 'Let us work as if success depended upon ourselves alone; but with heartfelt conviction that we are doing nothing and God everything.'

ST JUSTIN MARTYR
c.100–c.165

Lived: Flavia Neapolis, Palestine
Beard: Thick, white, ruddy
Claim: Raised as a pagan, he later converted and is seen as the first positive encounter of Christianity and Greek philosophy.
Quote: 'Is this not the task of philosophy, to enquire about the divine?'

ORIGEN
c.185–c.254

Lived: Alexandria, Egypt
Beard: White, thick, limp
Claim: Influential, but occasionally heretical teacher. Castrated himself so he could tutor women without suspicion.
Quote: 'The power of choosing good or evil is within the reach of all.'

ST POLYCARP
c.69–c.155

Lived: Smyrna, Turkey
Beard: Long, white, wild
Claim: One of the earliest Christian writers, he knew John the apostle. Patron saint of earache.
Quote: 'He who has char-ity is far from all sin.'

TERTULLIAN
c.160–c.225

Lived: Carthage, Tunisia
Beard: Short, white, festive
Claim: The first Christian theologian to write in Latin.
Quote: 'We multiply whenever we are mown down by you; the blood of Christians is seed.'

✳⟨ DATING EASTER SUNDAY ⟩✳

Easter – the celebration of the resurrection of Jesus – is a moveable feast, meaning it has no set date. When Easter was first established as an annual tradition it was based, as pagan festivals used to be, on the lunar calendar. Easter Sunday in the Western Church is thus on the first Sunday after the first full moon of the year to occur on or after the vernal equinox.

The year of this book's publication saw Easter Sunday fall on 23 March, the earliest it has been since 1913. Easter was also on 23 March in 1856 and 1845, but it hasn't been earlier than this date since 22 March 1818. It cannot fall earlier than 22 March.

An algorithm known as Carter's Method enables us to work out the date of any Easter between the years 1900 and 2099:

Calculate $D = 225 - 11(Y \bmod 19)$.

If D is greater than 50 then subtract multiples of 30 until the resulting new value of D is less than 51.

If D is greater than 48 subtract 1 from it.

Calculate $E = (Y + [Y/4] + D + 1) \bmod 7$ (NB Integer part of $[Y/4]$). Calculate $Q = D + 7 - E$.

If Q is less than 32 then Easter is in March.

If Q is greater than 31 then Q-31 is its date in April.

✠

But, if you're feeling lazy, the dates of Easter Sunday
for the next twenty-two years are:

2009 – 12 April	2020 – 12 April
2010 – 4 April	2021 – 4 April
2011 – 24 April	2022 – 17 April
2012 – 8 April	2023 – 9 April
2013 – 31 March	2024 – 31 March
2014 – 20 April	2025 – 20 April
2015 – 5 April	2026 – 5 April
2016 – 27 March	2027 – 28 March
2017 – 16 April	2028 – 16 April
2018 – 1 April	2029 – 1 April
2019 – 21 April	2030 – 21 April

✳{ THE GIFTS OF THE SPIRIT }✳

The Bible teaches that the Holy Spirit gives each of us different powers or abilities to be used for the common good. 1 Corinthians 12 lists nine 'gifts' of the Spirit.

Wisdom

Knowledge

Faith

Healing

Miraculous powers

Prophecy

Ability to distinguish between spirits

Speech in different tongues

Ability to interpret different tongues

✳{ THE FRUIT OF THE SPIRIT }✳

The Bible teaches that true virtues come not through our own efforts but by the working of the Holy Spirit in our lives. Galatians 5 lists the 'fruit' of the Spirit.

Love

Joy

Peace

Patience

Kindness

Goodness

Faithfulness

Gentleness

Self-control

⋇{ OLD MEN OF THE BIBLE }⋇

They built them to last in ancient days. The ten oldest people mentioned in the Bible were all born before the Great Flood. After the deluge, the average age seems to drop to below the 500-year mark and within a few generations Abraham dies at a sprightly 175 years old, yet it is described in the Bible as 'a good old age'. The top ten granddads are:

Methuselah – 969 years old

Jared – 962 years old

Noah – 950 years old

Adam – 930 years old

Seth – 912 years old

Kenan – 910 years old

Enosh – 905 years old

Mahalalel – 895 years old

Lamech – 777 years old

Shem – 600 years old

✢

Remember this:

*'Grey hair is a crown of splendour;
it is attained by a righteous life.'*

(Proverbs 16:31)

❊❨ Excommunicate! ❩❊

Excommunication is a state by which someone is excluded from spiritual and material benefits of being a baptised member of the Roman Catholic Church. There are various degrees of penalty:

- Being forbidden to administer or receive the sacraments.
- Being forbidden to share in or administer the Mass and other church services and prayers.
- Denial of a church burial.
- Denial of the jurisdiction of the Church, both to administer it or be subject to it.
- Being forbidden to acquire a benefice.
- Exile from church society.
- Exile from normal interaction with other members of the Church, including conversation, correspondence, business dealings and sharing meals or prayers.

AUTOMATIC EXCOMMUNICATION

There are seven offences for which the state of excommunication is automatically incurred upon a person:

- Being an apostate, heretic or schismatic, or for supporting or defending such a person.
- Desecrating or misusing the Eucharist.
- Using physical force against the Pope.
- (For a priest) Attempting to give absolution to someone with whom you have committed adultery.
- Consecrating a bishop without the Pope's authority.
- (For a priest) Violating the seal of confession.
- Procuring a successful abortion.

AVOIDING EXCOMMUNICATION

There are certain circumstances by which someone may commit one of the above offences and not be excommunicated:

- If the person is without full use of reason, for example a child or someone with a mental illness.
- If the person commits the offence under duress or overwhelming fear.
- If the person is ignorant of the laws and the penalties.

NAMED AND SHAMED

A less than exhaustive list of some of the Roman Catholic Church's higher-profile excommunications:

- *Holy Roman Emperors*: Henry IV, Henry V, Frederick II
- *British monarchs*: Henry II, Henry VIII, Elizabeth I
- *Other foreign leaders*: Robert the Bruce, Napoleon Bonaparte, Fidel Castro
- *Reformers*: Jan Hus, Martin Luther
- *Celebrities*: Joe DiMaggio, Sinead O'Connor

⁕⁊ WHAT IS LOVE? ⁊⁕

Does anybody love anybody anyway? Yes. And in 1 Corinthians 13 the Bible offers us a beautiful list of the attributes of true love, 'the most excellent way'.

Love is patient.

💜

Love is kind.

💜

Love does not envy, it does not boast, it is not proud.

💜

Love is not rude, it is not self-seeking, it is not easily angered, it keeps no record of wrongs.

💜

Love does not delight in evil but rejoices with the truth.

💜

Love always protects, always trusts, always hopes, always perseveres.

💜

Love never fails.

💜

⋇⟨ THE CIRCLES OF HELL ⟩⋇

Dante Alighieri's epic poem The Divine Comedy *charts the author's fictional exploration of hell, purgatory and heaven. He discovers hell divided into nine circles, at the centre of which sits Satan.*

THE FIRST CIRCLE

Otherwise known as Limbo, here reside those who were not sinful in life, but did not accept Christ.

THE SECOND CIRCLE
In this storm-ravaged circle suffer those who succumbed to the sin of lust.

THE THIRD CIRCLE

Guarded by the three-headed dog Cerberus, the gluttons are imprisoned in this circle of rain, snow and dirty slush.

THE FOURTH CIRCLE

The materially minded hoarders and wasters are here, guarded by the demon Plutus.

THE FIFTH CIRCLE

The River Styx covers this level. The souls of the wrathful fight each other in this sticky gloop, while the sullen and slothful lie concealed beneath its surface.

THE SIXTH CIRCLE

The walls of the city of Dis – a distorted version of the
heavenly New Jerusalem – stand on the threshold of the
sixth circle, in which the heretics burn in flaming tombs.

⊕

THE SEVENTH CIRCLE

A minotaur guards this circle, wherein reside the
souls of the violent, organised into three rings: those who
have been violent against other people, and property; those
who have been violent against themselves, including those
who have committed suicide; and those who have been
violent against God, art and nature.

⊕

THE EIGHTH CIRCLE

At the foot of a giant cliff, the eighth circle contains
the *Malebolge* – an arena of ten concentric ditches
entrapping various divisions of the souls of the fraudulent:
panderers and seducers; flatterers (sunk in excrement);
simonists (those who traded in spiritual blessings);
sorcerers and fortune tellers (whose heads are
twisted backwards on their bodies); barrators
(corrupt politicians); hypocrites; thieves; fraudulent
counsellors; sowers of discord; and falsifiers.

⊕

THE NINTH CIRCLE

The final circle is the frozen living tomb of the
treacherous, divided into four rings: *Caina*, named after
Cain, for traitors to their kin; *Antenora*, named after
Antenor of Troy, for traitors to their country; *Ptolomea*,

named after Ptolemy, for traitors to their guests; and *Judecca*, named after Judas Iscariot; for traitors to their masters. Sitting frozen to the waist in the very centre of the ninth circle, and so of hell itself, is Satan.

And the American satirical magazine *The Onion* reported in 1998 that a Tenth Circle had been constructed in hell. The Blockbuster Video-sponsored *Corpadverticus* circle would house a new breed of sinner: '"Demographers, advertising executives, tobacco lobbyists, monopoly-law experts retained by major corporations, and creators of office-based sitcoms – these new arrivals represent a wave of spiritual decay and horror the likes of which hell has never before seen," Inferno spokesman Antedeus said.'

'Faith is a living and unshakable confidence, a belief in God so assured that a man would die a thousand deaths for its sake.'

Martin Luther

⁎⟨ IT'S IN THE BIBLE ⟩⁎

It is often surprising to realise how many of our phrases in common use today are derived from the Bible. Here is but a small selection, with the biblical verse from which they derive (I have quoted from the King James Version of the Bible as it was from the earliest editions of this that most of these phrases will have slipped into everyday English usage).

Go forth and multiply

'God said unto them, "Be fruitful, and multiply, and replenish the earth"'. (Genesis 1:28)

✢

Off to the land of Nod

'And Cain went out from the presence of the Lord, and dwelt in the land of Nod, on the east of Eden'. (Genesis 4:16)

✢

The apple of his eye

'He found him in a desert land, and in the waste howling wilderness; he led him about, he instructed him, he kept him as the apple of his eye'. (Deuteronomy 32:10; also Psalm 17:8 and Proverbs 7:2)

✢

O, how the mighty are fallen

'How are the mighty fallen, and the weapons of war perished'. (2 Samuel 1:25)

✢

Gird up your loins

'And the hand of the Lord was on Elijah; and he girded up his loins, and ran before Ahab to the entrance of Jezreel'. (1 Kings 18:45)

✤

Out of the mouths of babes

'Out of the mouths of babes and sucklings hast thou ordained strength because of thine enemies'. (Psalm 8:2)

✤

Pride comes before a fall

'Pride goeth before destruction, and an haughty spirit before a fall'. (Proverbs 16:18)

✤

There's nothing new under the sun

'The thing that hath been, it is that which shall be; and that which is done is that which shall be done: and there is no new thing under the sun'. (Ecclesiastes 1:9)

✤

There is a time and a place for everything

'To every thing there is a season, and a time to every purpose under the heaven'. (Ecclesiastes 3:1)

✤

Putting a fly in the ointment

'Dead flies cause the ointment of the apothecary to send forth a stinking savour'. (Ecclesiastes 10:1)

To the four corners of the earth

'And he shall set up an ensign for the nations, and shall assemble the outcasts of Israel, and gather together the dispersed of Judah from the four corners of the earth'. (Isaiah 11:12)

✣

A leopard cannot change its spots

'Can the Ethiopian change his skin, or the leopard his spots?'. (Jeremiah 13:23)

✣

Found wanting

'Thou art weighed in the balances; and art found wanting'. (Daniel 5:27)

✣

Separating the wheat from the chaff

'He will thoroughly purge his floor, and gather up his wheat into the garner; but he will burn up the chaff with his unquenchable fire'. (Matthew 3:12)

✣

Don't hide your light under a bushel

'Neither do men light a candle, and put it under a bushel, but on a candlestick; and it giveth light unto all that are in the house'. (Matthew 5:15)

✣

His left hand doesn't know what his right hand is doing

'But when thou doest alms, let not thy left hand know what thy right hand doeth'. (Matthew 6:3)

✣

Casting pearls before swine

'Give not that which is holy unto the dogs, neither cast ye your pearls before swine, lest they trample them under their feet, and turn again and rend you'. (Matthew 7:6)

✣

The blind leading the blind

'Let them alone: they be blind leaders of the blind. And if the blind lead the blind, both shall fall into the ditch'. (Matthew 15:14)

✣

It's a sign of the times

'O ye hypocrites, ye can discern the face of the sky; but can ye not discern the signs of the times?'. (Matthew 16:3)

✣

He who lives by the sword, dies by the sword

'Put up again thy sword into his place: for all they that take the sword shall perish with the sword'. (Matthew 26:52)

✣

Physician, heal thyself

'Physician, heal thyself: whatsoever we have heard done in Capernaum, do also here in thy country'. (Luke 4:23)

Through a glass, darkly

'For now we see through a glass, darkly; but then face to face: now I know in part; but then shall I know even as I am known'. (1 Corinthians 13:12)

✣

Don't let the sun go down on your wrath

'Be ye angry, and sin not: let not the sun go down upon your wrath'. (Ephesians 4:26)

✣

Money is the root of all evil

Contrary to received wisdom, the actual verse is: 'For the *love* of money is the root of all evil: which while some coveted after, they have erred from the faith, and pierced themselves through with many sorrows'. (emphasis added, 1 Timothy 6:10)

⁎⟨ comedy vicars ⟩⁎

From the days of Chaucer, Shakespeare and Austen, men and women
of the cloth have always provided great comedy characters. Here are
ten of the best from the worlds of television and film.

REVEREND GERALDINE GRANGER
Played by Dawn French, *The Vicar of Dibley*

Reverend Geraldine Granger: *You were expecting a bloke …*
  beard, Bible, bad breath?
David Horton: *Yes, that sort of thing.*
Reverend Geraldine Granger: *Yeah. And instead, you got a*
  babe with a bob cut and a magnificent bosom.

❋

REVEREND LOVEJOY
Voiced by Harry Shearer, *The Simpsons*

Ned, have you considered any of the other major religions?
They're all pretty much the same.

❋

THE VICAR
Played by Dick Emery, *The Dick Emery Show*

Vicar: *On behalf of my flock I have been keeping a critical eye*
  on some of the scandalous strip clubs in the neighbourhood.
Interviewer: *And what are your conclusions?*
Vicar: *Well, for my money you can't whack Miss Lulu and her*
  trained python at the Girlies Galore.

❋

BRIAN HOPE AND CHARLIE McMANUS
Played by Eric Idle (Sr Inviolata of the Immaculate Conception) and
Robbie Coltrane (Sr Euphemia of the Five Wounds), *Nuns on the Run*

Brian Hope: *Let me try and summarise this: God is his son.
And his son is God. But his son moonlights as a holy ghost, a
holy spirit, and a dove. And they all send each other, even
though they're all one and the same thing.*
Charlie McManus: *You've got it. You really could be a nun!*

✹

FATHER TED AND FATHER DOUGAL
Played by Dermot Morgan and Ardal O'Hanlon, *Father Ted*

Father Dougal: *God, Ted, I heard about those cults. Everyone
dressing in black and saying our Lord's gonna come back
and judge us all!*
Father Ted: *No ... No, Dougal, that's us. That's Catholicism.*

✹

THE IMPRESSIVE CLERGYMAN
Played by Peter Cook, *The Princess Bride*

*Mawage. Mawage is wot bwings us togeder tooday. Mawage,
that bweffed awangment, that dweam wifin a dweam.*

✹

REVEREND MERVYN NOOTE
Played by Derek Nimmo, *All Gas and Gaiters*

The same actor played similar hapless clergymen in *Oh
Brother!*, *Oh Father!* and *Hell's Bells*.

✹

FATHER GERALD

Played by Rowan Atkinson, *Four Weddings and a Funeral*

In the name of the Father, the Son and the Holy Goat. Er, Ghost!

❋

FATHER FRANCIS MULCAHY

Played by William Christopher, *M*A*S*H*

Look on the bright side – when they tell us to serve our time in Purgatory, we can say, 'No thanks, I've done mine.'

❋

REVEREND ARTHUR BELLING

Played by Graham Chapman, *Monty Python's Flying Circus*

You know, there are many people in the country today who, through no fault of their own, are sane. Some of them were born sane; some of them became sane later in their lives. It is up to people, like you and me, who are out of our tiny little minds, to try and help these people overcome their sanity. You can start in small ways with ping pong ball eyes and a funny voice, and then you can paint half of your body red and the other half green, and then you can jump up and down in a bowl of treacle going 'SQUAWK SQUAWK SQUAWK SQUAWK SQUAWK!', and then you can go 'NERRR NERRR NERRR', and then you can roll around on the floor going 'PTING PTING PTING PTING PTING!'

⁎⟩ THE GNOSTIC GOSPELS ⟨⁎

Gnosticism was a wide, diverse movement of sects and belief systems that flourished in the 1st and 2nd centuries as they began to incorporate some of the ideas of the new religion, Christianity. Fundamental differences from the early church included the belief that we could be reunited with the heavenly state through the possession and understanding of gnosis *– secret knowledge. The Christ, or Saviour, came to help free us from the ignorance that bonded us to the material world, and Jesus of Nazareth was the man whose body this divine entity inhabited on earth, rather than God himself.*

The movement, particularly under the teaching and influence of leaders such as Simon the Magician (who is mentioned in the Bible – Acts 8:9–25), Basilides and Valentinus, was soon large enough to become a significant threat to the fledgling Church, and it was in the fires of ideological battle against these 'heresies' that Christians such as Irenaeus, Tertullian and Origen forged the principal theological tenets of what we recognise as orthodox Christianity today.

Knowledge of the Gnostics was limited until the last century, when several key writings were discovered. The most significant of these are known as the Gnostic Gospels.

THE GOSPEL OF THOMAS

Essentially a collection of sayings attributed to Jesus, as apparently recorded by the apostle Thomas, although the only version we have has probably been heavily edited from a Gnostic point of view. It suggests that understanding and embracing the teaching of Jesus at the deepest level of our beings can bring spiritual perfection and escape from death. We also need to transcend the divisions of the world, including male and female: 'Every female who makes herself male will enter heaven's kingdom.'

THE GOSPEL OF MARY

More than half this document is still missing but it seems to comprise dialogue between Jesus, the apostles and Mary Magdalene in the aftermath of Jesus' resurrection. There is lively debate, particularly between Mary and Peter, but she seems to have much more authority within the group than we glean from her few appearances in the Bible. Teaching includes the suggestion that we can be freed from sin by turning away from the physical world towards God, rather than through atonement.

THE GOSPEL OF THE EGYPTIANS

The actual title of this document is The Holy Book of the Great Invisible Spirit. It presents a detailed hierarchy of the heavens and the earth and rewrites the origin story of Judeo-Christian tradition. A series of powers emanate from the unknowable 'Divine Parent'; at the highest level is the group of three – Father, Mother and Son – and from these come the Christ, Adamus (the first human, a spiritual precursor to Adam), his son Seth (who fathers the human race) and various other spiritual luminaries.

THE GOSPEL OF TRUTH

One of the most widely disseminated Gnostic texts, this became foundational to the Valentinian sect of Gnosticism and was perhaps harder for the Church to suppress because of its allegorical nature. It emphasises that it is through knowledge we can achieve salvation.

THE GOSPEL OF PHILIP

A collection of Gnostic teachings and reflections which gives us insight on the rituals and sacramental worship of the Valentinians. This document has attracted most controversy for its suggestion that the relationship between Jesus and Mary Magdalene was more than platonic. It is said he loved her more than any other disciple and even kissed her on the mouth. Clearer understanding of Valentinian culture suggests a kiss on the mouth signified a kiss of peace or fellowship, so the reference was probably not meant to imply a sexual or romantic relationship.

THE GOSPEL OF JUDAS

This document, discovered as recently as 1978, relates a conversation between Jesus and his apostles in which he tells them that true knowledge is beyond them and only Judas is privileged to receive gnosis secrets from Jesus, who enlists Judas' help to free the spiritual Christ from within him (by betraying him so he may be executed). This elevates Judas to a much higher level than the other apostles – history's unfortunate scapegoat in contrast to his contemporaries who, through ignorance, failed to understand Jesus at such an intimate level and went on to build the legalistic institution of the Church which the Gnostics believed was leading people away from the truth.

❧ Trades of the Bible ❧

Kings, priests and prophets, carpenters, tax-collectors and fishermen ... Some of the professions of the Bible are familiar to us, but there is a far richer tapestry of crafts and trades recorded in the Scriptures.

ARMY

The geographical location of Israel has made the existence of a strong army a constant necessity. Every adult male in the tribes of Israel was expected to serve in the military.

...

BRICKMAKING

Exodus 1:14 – Making, firing and glazing bricks was one of the labour-intensive tasks the Israelites were forced to undertake during their captivity in Egypt.

...

GLASSMAKING

Deuteronomy 33:19 – When blessing Zebulun, Moses spoke of 'treasures hidden in the sand', which some believe to be a reference to making glass out of sand.

...

LAUNDRY

Malachi 3:2 – The fuller or launderer played an important role, particularly as part of the weaving industry.

...

LINENWORK

1 Chronicles 4:21 – Particular clans were associated with different trades, such as the fine linen workers of the families of Ashbea.

MUSIC

Psalm 68:25 – Music played a prominent part in the religious life of Israel in Bible times.

...

POTTERY

1 Chronicles 4:23 – A very important craft, not least for the making of water jars and other containers.

...

PROSTITUTION

Joshua 2:1 – The 'oldest profession' is at least as old as early biblical times, as evidenced by several mentions of prostitutes such as Rahab.

...

TANNING

Acts 9:43 – Tanning was a difficult trade for Jews, as it involved regular contact with the skins of dead animals, unclean under Jewish law, so its practitioners were often outcasts.

...

TENTMAKING

Acts 18:3 – In Old Testament times, tents were made of coarse animal skins, but by the time of Paul they were made of Cicilian cloth. Tentmaking was a skill passed down from the many years before the Israelites had a land of their own.

❧ An Unbroken Habit ❧

Monasticism is probably the aspect of contemporary Christian life which has changed least in the 2000-year history of the Church, and the contemplative life – while demanding – retains a deep attraction for many people in our materialistic world. Here are some of the best-known orders of monks and nuns.

AUGUSTINIANS
The Order of St Augustine

Founded: 1256, Italy
Life: Follow the Rule of St Augustine of Hippo (c.400). Pursuit of faith through learning.
Famous brothers: Martin Luther, Thomas à Kempis

BENEDICTINES
The Order of St Benedict

Founded: 529, Italy
Life: Follow the Rule of St Benedict of Nursia (c.529). Prayer, work and peace.
Famous brother: The Venerable Bede

CARMELITES
The Order of the Brothers of Our Lady of Mount Carmel

Founded: c.1154, Palestine
Life: Follow the Rule of St Albert (1209). Solitude, poverty and contemplative prayer.
Famous brother and sister: St John of the Cross, St Thérèse of Lisieux

CARTHUSIANS
The Carthusian Order. The Order of St Bruno

Founded: 1084, France
Life: Follow the Carthusian Rule (1127). Silence, meditation and
study.
Famous brother: Sir Thomas More

CISTERCIANS
The Order of Cistercians. White Monks

Founded: 1098, France
Life: Follow a stricter form of the Benedictine Rule. Secluded
community, manual labour and austerity.
Famous brother: St Bernard of Clairvaux

DOMINICANS
The Order of Preachers. Also known as Blackfriars

Founded: 1214, France
Life: The Augustinian Rule, with an emphasis on the intellectual
disciplines of preaching and study.
Famous brothers and sister: St Thomas Aquinas, Meister Eckhart,
Tomás de Torquemada, St Catherine of Siena

FRANCISCANS
The Orders of Friars Minor. Also known as Greyfriars.
Franciscan nuns are The Order of Poor Ladies, or the Poor Clares

Founded: 1209, Italy
Life: Follow the Rule of St Francis of Assisi, now lost. Complete
poverty, devotion, preaching.
Famous brother: Padre Pio

JESUITS
The Society of Jesus

Founded: 1540, France
Life: Spiritual life based on the Spiritual Exercises of St Ignatius
of Loyola, which train in the disciplines of meditation, prayer
and mental exercise. Missionary work and intellectual rigour.
Famous brother: St Francis Xavier

SERVITES
The Servite Friars. Servants of Mary

Founded: 1233, Italy
Life: The Augustinian Rule, with some Dominican additions.
Care of the poor and sick, and education.
Famous brother: St Philip Benizi

TRAPPISTS
The Order of Cistercians of the Strict Observance

Founded: 1664, France
Life: A reformed order of the Cistercians. Contemplative silence,
poverty and very limited contact with the outside world.
Famous brother: Thomas Merton

❊❧ INSURRECTIONISTS AT SUNDOWN ❧❊

Selected differences between the American and British versions of the most recent English translation of the Bible, Today's New International Version. *Always check what you buy — there are several American editions available in the British market.*

PSALM 50:21

US: 'But I now *arraign you* and set my accusations before you.'

British: 'But I now *bring you to court* and set my accusations before you.'

PROVERBS 30:29—31

US: 'There are three things that are stately in their stride, four that move with stately bearing: a lion, mighty amongst beasts, who retreats before nothing; a strutting *rooster*, a he-goat, and a king secure against revolt.'

British: 'There are three things that are stately in their stride, four that move with stately bearing: a lion, mighty amongst beasts, who retreats before nothing; a strutting *cock*, a he-goat, and a king secure against revolt.'

DANIEL 6:14

US: 'When the king heard this, he was greatly distressed; he was determined to rescue Daniel and made every effort until *sundown* to save him.'

British: 'When the king heard this, he was greatly distressed; he was determined to rescue Daniel and made every effort until *sunset* to save him.'

MATTHEW 3:10

US: 'The *ax is already at* the root of the trees, and every tree that does not produce good fruit will be cut down and thrown into the fire.'

British: 'The *axe has been laid to* the root of the trees, and every tree that does not produce good fruit will be cut down and thrown into the fire.'

MATTHEW 3:10

US: 'Then they *spit* in his face and struck him with their fists.'

British: 'Then they *spat* in his face and struck him with their fists.'

MATTHEW 3:10

US: 'A man called Barabbas was in prison with the *insurrectionists* who had committed murder in the uprising.'

British: 'A man called Barabbas was in prison with the *rebels* who had committed murder in the uprising.'

LUKE 2:11

US: 'Today in the town of David a *Savior* has been born to you; he is the Messiah, the Lord.'

British: 'Today in the town of David a *Saviour* has been born to you; he is the Messiah, the Lord.'

JOHN 4:29

US: 'Come, see a man who has told me everything *I ever did*. Could this be the Messiah?'

British: 'Come, see a man who has told me everything *I've ever done*. Could this be the Messiah?'

1 PETER 4:1

US: 'Therefore, since Christ suffered in his body, arm yourselves also with the same attitude, because those who have suffered in their bodies *are done* with sin.'

British: 'Therefore, since Christ suffered in his body, arm yourselves also with the same attitude, because those who have suffered in their bodies *have finished* with sin.'

REVELATION 6:8

US: 'They were given power over a *fourth* of the earth to kill by sword, famine and plague, and by the wild beasts of the earth.'

British: 'They were given power over a *quarter* of the earth to kill by sword, famine and plague, and by the wild beasts of the earth.'

'The Christian ideal has not been tried and found wanting. It has been found difficult and left untried.'

G. K. CHESTERTON

✧{ WHY GARGOYLE? }✧

'Gargoyle' is the term specifically reserved for gothic-style, sculpted outcrops on buildings – mainly churches and cathedrals – that house a spout to drain water away from the guttering, as opposed to other comically distorted carvings. Those without spouts are most likely chimeras *or* grotesques *and intended just for decoration.*

Gargoyles generally have the appearance of a demonic or mischievous creature (commonly dogs, pigs, cows, monkeys, lions, dragons, horses, bears, foxes or birds) or occasionally humans (monks, nuns, knights, children, saints and pilgrims). Sometimes two figures are compounded into one – a man protruding from the mouth of a dragon, for example.

They can be found on medieval church buildings all over Britain and across Europe although France is the real home of the gargoyle, and it was there that the odd little beasties became prolific during the gothic architectural revolution of the 12th, 13th and 14th centuries.

Beyond the purely functional purpose of directing corrosive rainwater away from the church structure and foundations, there are several theories on the reasons for gargoyles:

DECORATIONS

The Middle Ages saw a marked development in people's creative and imaginative faculties in Europe, and gargoyles were simply a decorative reflection of that trend.

BIBLICAL ILLUSTRATIONS

They are designed to reflect some of the vivid imagery of the Bible, such as Psalm 22:12–13 ('Many bulls have compassed me: strong bulls of Bashan have beset me round.

They gaped upon me with their mouths, as a ravening and a roaring lion') and Isaiah 11:8 ('And the suckling child shall play on the hole of the asp, and the weaned child shall put his hand on the cockatrice's den').

DINOSAURS

Some hold that medieval discoveries of traces of prehistoric creatures might also have sparked the visualisation of beasts such as gargoyles in art and popular storytelling.

TROPHIES

Gargoyles represent demons and devils, over whom God has the final victory, and are plastered over churches like a headhunter's trophies.

SCARECROWS

Conversely, the gargoyles are the church's protectors – warding off evil and malevolent spirits.

DEVOTIONS

As most gargoyles are placed near the top of churches, it has been suggested that sculptors wanted to place their best, most extravagant works closest to God for his approval.

MISCHIEF

Or were they simply a chance for the sculptor to be playful, at a height where most people would not be able to pick out the details of their creations? It is possible that some gargoyles are caricatures of members of the clergy or local community.

CHURCH CANDY

The Middle Ages was a period in which the Church in Europe sought to increase its numbers, and the gargoyles could have been an attempt to draw on pagan mythology to entice non-believers into church.

SUPERSTITION

Some say that builders believed a wall without a gargoyle on it would fall down.

A BIT OF A LAUGH

Some evidence suggests that the Church was not without a sense of fun in the Middle Ages – some of the mystery plays and festivals held within churches were particularly bawdy – and the principal purpose of gargoyles could simply have been to entertain the laity.

{ SAINTS R US }

A list of fifty-two patron saints — one for each week of the year.

Barbers — ST MARTIN DE PORRES
Bartenders — ST ARMAND
Beekeepers — ST AMBROSE
Birds — ST GALL
Blackbirds — ST KEVIN
Blood donors — OUR LADY OF THE THORNS
Broadcasters — THE ARCHANGEL GABRIEL
Bus drivers — ST CHRISTOPHER

Cab drivers — ST FIACRE
Café owners — ST DROGO
Cats — ST GERTRUDE
Chimney sweeps — ST FLORIAN
Clowns — ST GENESIUS
Comedians — ST VITUS
Cyclists — ST MADONNA OF GHISALLO

Disappointing children — ST CLOTILDE
Dogs — ST ROCHE

Falling (and jumping …) — ST VENANTIUS
Fish — ST NEOT
Funeral directors — JOAN OF ARC

Gravediggers — ST ANTHONY THE ABBOT

Haemorrhoid sufferers — ST FIACRE
Hangovers — ST VIVIAN
Hoarseness — ST BERNARDINE OF SIENA
House hunting — JOSEPH OF ARIMATHEA

Insect bites — ST MARK
Internet — ST ISIDORE OF SEVILLE

Lazy — ST LAWRENCE
Librarians — ST JEROME
Lighthouse keepers — ST VENERIUS

Marriages (happy) — ST VALENTINE
Marriages (unhappy) — ST GENGULF
Motorways — JOHN THE BAPTIST

Park-keepers — ST JOHN GUALBERT
Perfumers — MARY MAGDALENE
Postmen — ST GABRIEL THE ARCHANGEL
Psychiatrists — ST CHRISTINE THE ASTONISHING

The Really Ugly — ST DROGO

Servants who have broken their master's belongings — ST BENEDICT
Short-sighted — ST CLARUS
Skaters — ST LIDWINA OF SCHIEDAM
Skiers — ST BERNARD OF MONTJOUX
Sleepwalkers — ST DYMPHNA
Spelunkers — ST BENEDICT
Stamp collectors — THE ARCHANGEL GABRIEL
Storks — ST AGRICOLA OF AVIGNON

Television — ST CLARE
Toothache — ST APPOLONIA

Undertakers — JOSEPH OF ARIMATHEA

Vets — OUR LADY OF COROMOTO

Waitresses — ST MARTHA
Warehouses — ST BARBARA

✤ True Love Stories ✤

Mills and Boon have nothing on the Scriptures for affairs of the heart. Here are ten of the Bible's greatest romances. And not all of these lovers lived happily ever after ...

ADAM AND EVE

He was a lonely gardener. She brought him an apple.
The rest is history.

✤

ABRAHAM AND SARAH

He was one hundred. She was ninety. She bore him a son.
He fathered a nation.

✤

SAMSON AND DELILAH

He told her his darkest secret. She gave him a number one
buzz cut. He brought the house down.

✤

RUTH AND BOAZ

She was the beautiful young widow. He was the handsome
landowner. Their eyes met across a crowded field.

✤

DAVID AND BATHSHEBA

She took a bath while her husband was at war. He caught a
glimpse and wanted more. When they met, it was murder.

✤

JOB AND HER INDOORS

He sat in the ashes, scraped himself with broken pottery
and cried 'What's the point of it all?' She told him to get
real. He called her a foolish woman.

✣

LOVER AND BELOVED

She said he was radiant and ruddy, outstanding among ten
thousand, his head purest gold and his hair wavy and black
as a raven. He likened her to a mare. But he seemed to get
away with that one.

✣

AHAB AND JEZEBEL

He was the most evil, murderous ruler of his age. She was
no better. When they died, dogs licked their blood from
the streets.

✣

ZECHARIAH AND ELIZABETH

He was a priest who questioned God's blessing. She gave
birth to one of the greatest prophets. He was lost for words.

✣

MARY AND JOSEPH

He was a carpenter. She was a virgin. Together, they
protected and raised the Son of God.

⁎{ WHAT MILLENNIALIST AM I? }⁎

The twentieth chapter of the book of Revelation, a prophetic vision revealed through the apostle John, is believed to predict the turbulent events surrounding the Second Coming of Jesus Christ and his final victory over Satan. There is talk of a period of one thousand years, a mighty battle between Good and Evil, and the resurrection and judgement of the dead. But there are many different interpretations of the passage and the precise sequence of events being foretold.

What do *you* believe?

1. That Jesus' Second Coming will follow the breakdown of society into immorality and despair, and the rise of a single global kingdom or government of evil. The thousand years of Revelation 20 will be under Jesus' rule, following his return, and will eventually end with the Last Judgement of the Dead. If yes, then you are a variety of *Premillennialist* – go straight to question 4.

2. That Jesus' Second Coming, and with it the Last Judgement, comes *after* the thousand-year period, heralded by the efforts of the faithful on earth. If yes, then proceed to question 6, and discover just what flavour of *Postmillennialist* you are.

3. That the thousand years in John's prophecy should not be interpreted literally, but are a figurative description of the age we are in now – the period between Jesus' First Coming and Second Coming. Evil will continue to grow in power on the earth, until the Last Judgement when Jesus returns. If yes, then wonder no more – you are an *Amillennialist*.

4. Do you believe that we all suffer the period of tribulation – in which Satan grows in power and persecutes those who stand against him? That this time will end when the faithful are drawn up from earth in a great rapture to share Jesus' triumphal return? If yes, then congratulations – you are a *Post-tribulational Premillennialist*.

5. Do you believe that the rapture of the faithful will take place *before* the tribulation and the short rule of the Antichrist? That Jesus will return with the raptured Christians to claim his victory and the start of his great millennial rule? If yes, then you are *Pretribulational Premillennialist* (or *Dispensational Premillennialist* if you want to sound flash).

6. Do you believe that the thousand years preceding Jesus' return is a time (the thousand years possibly figurative, not literal) of gradual Christian revival across the world, ushering in his final victory? If yes, then that makes you a *Revivalist Postmillennialist*.

7. Do you believe that the thousand years is a period in which the Church rules the earth before Jesus' return, and will only begin *after* a period of successful Christian revival? If yes, then you will be delighted to learn you are a *Reconstructionist Postmillennialist*.

∗{ CHILDREN OF THE BIBLE }∗

Possibly because they appealed to us most when we first heard them as youngsters ourselves, some of the Bible's most memorable stories concern children.

There are very few girls named in the Bible because of the culture in which it was written. Jesus' mother Mary is one of the youngest named – she is popularly believed to have been around fourteen when visited by the angel Gabriel, although she probably would not have been considered a child at the time.

ISHMAEL AND ISAAC

Ishmael was the first son of Abraham, born to his wife Sarah's Egyptian servant Hagar, because Sarah herself was barren. But God eventually blessed Abraham and Sarah with a son, Isaac. Ishmael jealously teased his stepbrother and, after being sent away by his father, became an archer in the desert. Isaac inherited the birthright of Abraham's covenant with God.

...

ESAU AND JACOB

Isaac's own sons were similarly ill-matched. Non-identical twins – Esau was red and hairy, Jacob 'smooth-skinned' – the latter was born holding on to Esau's heel, and would grow up to claim his brother's birthright.

...

MOSES

To protect him from the Egyptian cull of newborn Israelite boys, Moses' mother hid him in a basket among the reeds of the River Nile when he was just three months

old. He was discovered by Pharaoh's daughter and grew
up in the Egyptian royal household, although he would
eventually lead the Israelites to liberation.

...

SAMUEL

Given by his mother to serve in the Temple as a young
boy – although she visited him regularly and brought him a
new robe once a year – Samuel grew up close to God and
was soon recognised as a mighty prophet by all of Israel.

...

DAVID

Ruddy-faced, handsome and athletic, talented as
both musician and warrior, David was the youngest son of
Jesse. Called from his shepherding duties and anointed
with God's Spirit, he became a legend by defeating the
mighty Philistine Goliath.

...

NAAMAN'S MAID

A young Israelite girl, kidnapped by the Arameans
and serving as a maid in the household of the soldier
Naaman, showed faith and compassion when she suggested
her master visit the prophet Elisha to be healed of leprosy.

...

JOASH

At the age of seven, Joash became the youngest
king of Judah, having spent the previous six years in
hiding from his murderous grandmother Athaliah.
His great, great, great, great grandson Manasseh
became king at the age of twelve, and *his* grandson
Josiah came to the throne aged eight.

JESUS

Compared to accounts of his adult ministry we are told little about the childhood of Jesus apart from the dramatic story of his birth and subsequent flight to Egypt to escape the wrath of King Herod, and his visit to the Temple in Jerusalem at the age of twelve, when he slipped away from his parents and was discovered after three days, sitting among the teachers and demonstrating astonishing knowledge of the Scriptures.

...

JESUS AND THE CHILDREN

Children feature fairly prominently in Jesus' ministry, both in his interactions and in his teaching. One of the most astonishing of his miracles, recorded in all three of the Synoptic Gospels, was the bringing to life of a twelve-year-old girl, the daughter of synagogue ruler Jairus. Later, when Jesus exposed the hypocrisy of the temple traders, he excited a crowd of children who shouted his praises – to the indignation of the priests. Jesus famously taught: 'Let the little children come to me, and do not hinder them, for the kingdom of heaven belongs to such as these.'

...

And the Bible's youngest of them all is John the Baptist who, true to his excitable nature, leaped in his mother Elizabeth's womb!

⁎❳ Ten Popular Mealtime Graces ❲⁎

*Many Christian households – and some non-Christian ones too –
have a favourite form of words for giving thanks before a meal.
Sometimes it is one remembered from school or one's own parents,
and sometimes something brisk and modern to capture the children's interest. Here are ten of the most popular, traditional and
contemporary.*

Give us grateful hearts, O Father, for all thy mercies, and
make us mindful of the needs of others; through Jesus
Christ our Lord. Amen.

'Book of Common Prayer', 1928

Some hae meat and canna eat,
And some wad eat that want it;
But we hae meat, and we can eat,
Sae let the Lord be thankit.

'The Selkirk Grace', by Robert Burns

Bless us, O Lord, and these thy gifts, which we are about to
receive from thy bounty, through Christ our Lord.
Amen.
Benedic, Domine, nos et haec tua dona quae de tua largi-
tate sumus sumpturi. Per Christum Dominum nostrum.
Amen.

Traditional Roman Catholic prayer, in English and Latin

The poor shall eat and be satisfied, and those who seek the
Lord shall praise him; their hearts shall live forever!
Glory to the Father, and to the Son, and to the Holy Spirit,
now and ever and unto ages of ages. Amen.
Lord, have mercy! Lord, have mercy! Lord, have mercy!
O Christ God, bless the food and drink of thy servants, for
thou art holy, always, now and ever and unto ages of ages.
Amen.

Traditional Orthodox prayer

God bless us [hands on head]
God bless the food [hands around the plate]
Amen. [hands folded]

For bacon, eggs and buttered toast,
Praise Father, Son and Holy Ghost.

For what we are about to receive,
may the Lord make us truly thankful.
Amen.

For good food and those who prepare it,
For good friends with whom to share it,
We thank you, Lord. Amen.

Thank you for the food we eat,
Thank you for the world so sweet,
Thank you for the birds that sing,
Thank you God for everything.

Bless the bunch that munch this lunch.

*'What is the chief end of man? To glorify God
and to enjoy him for ever.'*

THE SHORTER CATECHISM, 1647

✵⟩ THE APOSTLES' CREED ⟨✵

*Legend has it that, in the face of scattergun theological teaching
from 1st-century Gnostics, the twelve apostles united under the
influence of the Holy Spirit at Pentecost to create the Apostles' Creed
— a unifying statement of faith still used in many churches today.
It is said that each apostle dictated one part of it.*

PETER:

*I believe in One God, Father Almighty,
maker of heaven and earth*

ANDREW:

And in Jesus Christ his only son our Lord

JAMES (SON OF ZEBEDEE):

*Who was conceived of the Holy Spirit,
born of the Virgin Mary*

JOHN:

*Suffered under Pontius Pilate, was crucified,
died and was buried*

THOMAS:

*He descended into hell; on the third day he
rose again from the dead*

JAMES (SON OF ALPHAEUS):

*He ascended into heaven and he sits at the right
hand of God the Father Almighty*

PHILIP:

From thence he shall come to judge the living and the dead

BARTHOLOMEW:

I believe in the Holy Spirit

MATTHEW:

The Holy Catholic Church, the communion of saints

SIMON THE ZEALOT:

The forgiveness of sins

JUDE:

The resurrection of the body

MATTHIAS:

And the life everlasting. Amen.

❧ HYMN LORE ❧

Some curious facts about hymns.

OLDEST HYMN OF WHICH WE KNOW THE AUTHOR

'Shepherd of Tender' Youth by St Clement of Alexandria
(c.150–c.211), translated from Greek to English
by Henry Dexter in 1846.

❖

FIRST HYMN WRITTEN IN ENGLISH FOR PUBLIC WORSHIP

'All People that on Earth do Dwell', written by
William Kethe and published in 1561. This hymn, still
popular today, was a paraphrase of Psalm 100.
'Behold the Glories of the Lamb', which was written by
Isaac Watts around 1688, is believed to be the first
non-Psalm-based English hymn to be sung in church.

❖

HYMNS WHOSE AUTHORS NEVER HEARD THEM SUNG

'Abide with me', completed by Henry Lyte in 1847,
on the day before he travelled to Italy to try to recover
from tuberculosis. Sadly, he died en route.
'I will Sing of my Redeemer'. The words were discovered in
the luggage of American writer Philip Bliss after he died in
a train crash in Ohio in 1876. Bliss survived the initial
crash, caused by a bridge collapse, but perished in the
flames when he went back to try to rescue his wife.

❖

HYMNS THAT FIRST APPEARED IN NOVELS

'Jesus Loves Me, This I Know'. Written in 1860 by
Anna Warner, for her sister Susan Warner's novel
Say and Seal. Susan needed a song for a Sunday
school teacher to sing to a dying boy.
'When Israel, of the Lord Beloved'. In Walter Scott's
Ivanhoe (1817), the healer Rebecca, a Jew, sings this hymn
in prison after being sentenced to death for sorcery.

MOST PROLIFIC AUTHOR OF HYMNS

This is believed to be *Frances (Fanny) Crosby* (1820–1915),
who wrote over 8000 hymns under at least 200
pseudonyms, despite being blind from the age of six
weeks (as a result of her doctor applying a mustard poultice
to her forehead to try and cure a cold). She wrote her last
hymn at the age of ninety-five, the day before she died.
Charles Wesley wrote over 6000 hymns.

*'A Christian should always remember that the
value of his good works is not based on their
number and excellence, but on the love of God
which prompts him to do these things.'*

St John of the Cross

⁕⁊ sacred numbers ⁊⁕

The following numbers have recurring meanings in traditional Christian art and literature.

1

God: the first and all-encompassing
Unity: of God and of the Church

2

God the Father and God the Son
The humanity and divinity of Jesus
The material and the spiritual
The Old and New Testaments

3

The Trinity: God the Father, God the Son and God the
   Holy Spirit
Jesus' three days in the tomb
The three epochs of humanity: before the law (Adam to
   Moses), under the law (Moses to Jesus), under grace
   (Jesus to the Last Judgement)
The three greatest gifts: faith, hope and love

4

The four evangelists: Matthew, Mark, Luke and John
The cross: four extremities
The earth, which has four corners and four seasons

5

The cross: four extremities plus cross-section
Sacrifice: the five wounds received by Jesus on the cross
(hands, feet and side), and replicated in the stigmata of
St Francis of Assisi

6

Creation: the number of days in which God created the earth
Imperfection: being one short of seven, the number of
perfection

7

Perfection: God rested and admired his work on the seventh
day
Virtues: Chastity, Temperance, Charity, Diligence,
Patience, Kindness, Humility
Sins: Lust, Gluttony, Greed, Sloth, Wrath, Envy, Pride

8

Jesus: an octagon is halfway between a circle (God) and a
square (earth), just as Jesus mediates between us and
God
Baptism and rebirth: Jesus rose from the dead eight days
after entering Jerusalem

9

Angels: the nine choirs of angels (Cherubim, Seraphim,
Ophanim, Thrones, Dominions, Powers, Principalities,
Archangels, Angels)

10

The Ten Commandments

12

The Church: complete, as are the twelve apostles and the twelve tribes of Israel

13

Betrayal: the number of people at the Last Supper

40

Trial or testing: the number of years the Israelites travelled in the desert, and the number of days of the Great Flood and Jesus' temptation in the wilderness.

⁂

'If the works of God were such as might be easily comprehended by human reason, they could not be called wonderful or unspeakable.'

Thomas À Kempis

{ WHO DO YOU SAY I AM? }

As the relentless task of translating the Bible into all the world's languages continues (see 'The Word for All'), the name of Jesus is constantly spoken by new tongues. Here are some of the many different translations of his name:

AZEZI
Farefare (Ghana)

•••

HESU
Querétaro Otomie (Mexico)

•••

IESU
Korafe, Ömie (both Papua New Guinea), Tangoa (Vanuatu)

•••

IESUS
Nakanai (Papua New Guinea)

•••

IHU
North Tairora (Papua New Guinea)

•••

ISA
Arabic (Middle East, North Africa and other Muslim countries)

•••

ÎTU
Usarufa (Papua New Guinea)

•••

JESO
Duruma (Kenya)

•••

JESU
Adioukrou (Ivory Coast), Barai (Papua New Guinea), Guanano (Brazil)

JESUSE
Zinacantán Tzotzil (Mexico)

•••

JESUU
Coatzospan Mixtec (Mexico)

•••

JISAS
Abau, Alamblak, Amele, Angaataha, Bukiyip, Mufian,
Safeyoka (all Papua New Guinea)

•••

SISA
Awa (Papua New Guinea)

•••

XESOSI
Apurinã (Brazil)

•••

YA:SU
Aramia River Tabo, Fly River Tabo (both Papua New Guinea)

•••

YEESU
South Fali (Cameroon)

•••

YESU
Bunama, Dedua (both Papua New Guinea), Korean
(North and South Korea), Longuda (Nigeria), Mündü (Sudan),
Swahili (Tanzania, Rwanda, Kenya, Uganda),
Southwest Tanna (Vanuatu)

•••

YESUS
Kauili Da'a (Indonesia)

•••

YIISA
Bimoba (Ghana)

YIITJU
Pintupi-Luritja (Australia)

•••

YUSU
Plapo Krumen (Ivory Coast)

•••

ZESU
Mwan (Ivory Coast)

'The Christian should resemble a fruit tree, not a Christmas tree! For the gaudy decorations of a Christmas tree are only tied on, whereas fruit grows on a fruit tree.'

JOHN STOTT

✲⟩ BOYS' CHRISTIAN NAMES ⟨✲

The term 'Christian name' is used in an official context less fre-
quently than 'first name' or even 'given name' these days, although
these lists of the most popular UK names of recent years and at
regular intervals throughout the last century suggest that biblical
names are still favoured for boys, if less so for girls.

2007
1 JACK .... The name Jack dates to the Middle Ages
2 THOMAS   and is derived from the name John (see
3 OLIVER   below). It has been the UK's most popular
                   Christian name since 1995.

2006	2005	2004
1 JACK	1 JACK	1 JACK
2 THOMAS	2 JOSHUA	2 JOSHUA
3 JOSHUA	3 THOMAS	3 THOMAS

1994
1 THOMAS .... Derived from the Aramaic *Tom* meaning
2 JAMES   'twin', the biblical designation of the
3 JACK   apostle Thomas.

1984
1 CHRISTOPHER ········· Derived from Ancient Greek, meaning
2 JAMES   'bearer of the anointed one (Christ)'.
3 DAVID   The legend of St Christopher tells of him
                 carrying the young Jesus across a river.

1974

1 PAUL ·························· From the Latin meaning 'humble', this
2 MARK name has a strong Christian heritage in
3 DAVID the great 1st-century missionary and
prolific writer of New Testament epistles,
and six Pope Pauls (not to mention two
Pope John Pauls).

1964

1 DAVID ·························· A Hebrew name meaning 'beloved', its
2 PAUL popularity stems from the Old Testament
3 ANDREW David – the giant-slaying, Philistine-
conquering, harp-playing, psalm-writing
King of Israel.

1954

1 DAVID
2 JOHN
3 STEPHEN

1944

1 JOHN ·························· Derived from the Hebrew name *Yoannan*,
2 DAVID meaning 'God is gracious'. John the
3 MICHAEL Baptist announced Jesus as the Messiah,
and the apostle John is believed to have
written several books of the New
Testament.

1934	1924	1914
1 JOHN	1 JOHN	1 JOHN
2 PETER	2 WILLIAM	2 WILLIAM
3 WILLIAM	3 GEORGE	3 GEORGE

1904

1 WILLIAM ·················· A Germanic name, *wil* meaning 'desire'
2 JOHN and *helm* meaning 'helmet or protection'.
3 GEORGE It was popularised in English after
William the Conqueror, and either it or
John was the most popular first name for
boys in both England and the United
States every year for about 500 years
between the 16th and 20th centuries.

✤⟩ GIRLS' CHRISTIAN NAMES ⟨✤

2007

1 GRACE ············· From the Latin *gratia*, meaning 'favour'.
2 RUBY
3 OLIVIA
Grace as a theological term refers to God's free, unmerited gift to men and women: both blessing in everyday life and our ultimate salvation.

2006

1 OLIVIA ············· A Latin name, its first recorded English
2 GRACE
3 JESSICA
use was in Shakespeare's *Twelfth Night*. Possibly derived from the boy's name Oliver meaning 'bearer of the olive branch', a symbol of peace and goodwill. This reminds us of the dove that brought an olive leaf to Noah as a sign that the great flood was receding, although the symbolism predates Christian or Jewish tradition.

2005

1 JESSICA ············· Another name first recorded in
2 EMILY
3 SOPHIE
Shakespeare (*The Merchant of Venice*). It is possibly based on the Hebrew name *Iesca*, meaning foresight. The Bible names one of Abraham's nieces as Iesca.

2004

1 EMILY ············· Derived from the Germanic word *ermen*,
2 ELLIE
3 JESSICA
meaning 'whole' or 'universal'.

1994

1 REBECCA ·················· From Aramaic, or the Hebrew name
2 LAUREN   *Ribquah*, meaning 'to tie or bind' or
3 JESSICA   'captivating'. Rebekah was the wife of
                      Abraham's son Isaac, chosen because of
                      her kindness to a thirsty servant.

1984

1 SARAH ··················· Meaning 'woman of high rank' or
2 LAURA   'princess' in Hebrew. Sarah was the wife
3 GEMMA   of Abraham and, through their son Isaac,
                      mother of the Israelite nation blessed by
                      God. Before God's new covenant with her
                      husband, she was Sarai, which also means
                      woman of high rank but without such
                      grand anointing.

1974

1 SARAH
2 CLAIRE
3 NICOLA

1964

1 SUSAN ··················· A popular name with Persian roots,
2 JULIE   *sausan* meaning 'lily'.
3 KAREN

1954

1 SUSAN
2 LINDA
3 CHRISTINE

1944

1 MARGARET ⋯⋯⋯⋯⋯⋯ From the Greek *margarita*, meaning
2 PATRICIA   'pearl'. Margaret has been one of the
3 CHRISTINE   most popular English names since the
                    Middle Ages.

1934	1924
1 MARGARET	1 MARGARET
2 JEAN	2 MARY
3 MARY	3 JEAN

1914

1 MARY ⋯⋯⋯⋯⋯⋯⋯ Dating from the Hebrew *Miryam*, Mary
2 MARGARET   was a hugely popular Jewish name up to
3 DORIS   the time of Jesus but was considered too
                  sacred for use as a common first name for
                  hundreds of years after the life of his
                  mother. Its use in Britain began around
                  the 12th century and it became the num-
                  ber one girl's name for centuries after. It
                  is less popular now, although the name
                  Maria re-entered the top 100 girls' names
                  list in 2007.

1904

1 MARY
2 FLORENCE
3 DORIS

❊⟨ STOLES ⟩❊

The stole is a length of cloth draped over a priest's shoulders with its ends hanging down to his or her waist. A familiar sight to most of us, but did you know the colour of the stole is usually chosen according to the nature of the service or season of the church year?

WHITE

Worn for Easter, Christmas and feasts
(except martyrs' feasts)

RED

Worn for Palm Sunday, Good Friday, Pentecost
and feasts of martyred saints

GREEN

Worn for 'Ordinary Time' –
the season leading up to Advent

PURPLE

Worn for Advent and Lent

BLUE

Some clergy wear blue during Advent

PINK

Sometimes worn on the third Sunday in Advent and the
fourth Sunday in Lent

BLACK

Worn for funerals and masses for the dead

CRIMSON

Sometimes worn for Holy Week

*'A man can accept what Christ has done without
knowing how it works; indeed, he certainly won't
know how it works until he's accepted it.'*

C. S. Lewis

✠ THE PLAGUES OF EGYPT ✠

There are countless shocking stories in the Old Testament, but few as horrific as the series of plagues God inflicted on the nation of Egypt through Moses and Aaron — extreme measures which eventually forced Pharaoh to release the Israelites from oppression and slavery.

THE PLAGUE OF BLOOD

Aaron raised his staff and struck the water of the Nile, and all the water was changed into blood. The fish in the Nile died, and the river smelled so bad that the Egyptians could not drink its water. Blood was everywhere in Egypt.

THE PLAGUE OF FROGS

'They will come up into your palace and your bedroom and onto your bed, into the houses of your officials and on your people, and into your ovens and kneading troughs.'

THE PLAGUE OF GNATS

When Aaron stretched out his hand with the staff and struck the dust of the ground, gnats came upon men and animals. All the dust throughout the land of Egypt became gnats.

THE PLAGUE OF FLIES

Dense swarms of flies poured into Pharaoh's palace and into the houses of his officials, and throughout Egypt the land was ruined by the flies.

THE PLAGUE ON LIVESTOCK

All the livestock of the Egyptians died, but not one animal belonging to the Israelites died.

THE PLAGUE OF BOILS

Moses and Aaron took soot from a furnace and stood before Pharaoh. Moses tossed it into the air, and festering boils broke out on men and animals. The magicians could not stand before Moses because of the boils that were on them and on all the Egyptians.

THE PLAGUE OF HAIL

Hail fell and lightning flashed back and forth. It was the worst storm in all the land of Egypt since it had become a nation. Throughout Egypt hail struck everything in the fields – both men and animals; it beat down everything growing in the fields and stripped every tree.

THE PLAGUE OF LOCUSTS

The Lord made an east wind blow across the land all that day and all that night. By morning the wind had brought the locusts; they invaded all Egypt and settled down in every area of the country in great numbers. Never before had there been such a plague of locusts, nor will there ever be again. They covered the ground until it was black. They devoured all that was left after the hail – everything growing in the fields and the fruit on the trees. Nothing green remained on tree or plant in all the land of Egypt.

THE PLAGUE OF DARKNESS

Moses stretched out his hand towards the sky, and total darkness covered all Egypt for three days. No-one could see anyone else or leave his or her place for three days. Yet all the Israelites had light in the places where they lived.

THE PLAGUE ON THE FIRSTBORN

At midnight the Lord struck down all the firstborn in Egypt, from the firstborn of Pharaoh, who sat on the throne, to the firstborn of the prisoner, who was in the dungeon, and the firstborn of all the livestock as well. There was loud wailing in Egypt, for there was not a house without someone dead.

✳⟨ DATING THE BIBLE ⟩✳

The exact dates at which each book of the Bible was written are debated. Some, such as Isaiah, are placed at some point within the estimated period of the author's life and ministry. Others, such as the Psalms and Proverbs, were collected and compiled over many centuries. And so little is known of the authorship of others, including Job and Joel, that they are given dates many hundreds of years apart by different scholars. The table on the follwing pages is intended to give us an idea of where each sits on the timeline in relation to the others, rather than precise dates.

1500	1400	1300	1200	1100	1000	900	800	700	600	500	400

OLD TESTAMENT

Genesis
Exodus
Leviticus
Numbers
Deuteronomy
Joshua

Judges
Ruth
1 Samuel
2 Samuel
1 Kings
2 Kings
1 Chronicles
2 Chronicles
Ezra
Nehemiah
Esther
Job
Psalms

Proverbs
Ecclesiastes
Song of Songs
Isaiah
Jeremiah
Lamentations
Ezekiel
Daniel
Hosea
Joel
Amos
Obadiah
Jonah
Micah
Nahum
Habakkuk
Zephaniah
Haggai
Zechariah
Malachi

```
        300   200   100  BC | AD   10  100  30  200  50  60  70  80  90  100 110 120
```

Matthew
Mark
Luke
John
Acts
Romans
1 Corinthians
2 Corinthians

Galatians
Ephesians
Philippians
Colossians
1 Thessalonians
2 Thessalonians
1 Timothy
2 Timothy
Titus
Philemon
Hebrews

James
1 Peter
2 Peter
1 John
2 John
3 John
Jude
Revelation

NEW TESTAMENT

DEUTEROCANONICALS

Tobit
Judith
1 Maccabees
2 Maccabees
Wisdom
Ecclesiasticus
Baruch

⁕⟨ Know Your Church ⟩⁕

Some useful definitions of church furniture and architectural terms.

ALMONRY

The chamber in a church from which alms
were distributed to the poor.

CHANCEL (OR SANCTUARY)

The east wing of a church, sometimes enclosed, which
contains the altar and often the lectern, pulpit, credence
table and choir stalls.

CIBORIUM

A canopy supported on pillars above the altar.

CREDENCE TABLE

A small table kept on the south side of the chancel,
on which are kept items used in the celebration of
Holy Communion.

LADY CHAPEL

A chapel dedicated to the Virgin Mary inside a large
church or cathedral.

⊕

LYCHGATE

A small porch erected over the entrance gate to some churchyards, designed to give shelter to pallbearers before they entered the church at a funeral.

MISERICORD (OR MERCY SEAT)

A small shelf underneath folding seats in church, which offers support to people standing for long periods of prayer.

NARTHEX

The entrance area of a church traditionally situated at the west end of the nave, furthest from the altar.

NAVE

The pew-lined central aisle of the church providing the path between narthex and chancel.

ROOD SCREEN

A large, ornate screen that divides the nave from the chancel.

SACRISTY (OR VESTRY)

A separate room of the church, in which are stored vestments, church furniture and documents.

STOUP

A recessed bowl by the entrance of some churches containing holy water. People entering may dip their fingers in the water and cross themselves.

TRANSEPT

The north–south axis of a cross-shaped church, running between the nave and the entrance to the chancel.

'A Christian is a keyhole through which other folk see God.'

ROBERT E. GIBSON

❧ CURIOUS BIBLES ❧

The Bible is a remarkable book, packed with epic yarns, prophecies, history, parables and wisdom, written by many different writers over hundreds of years in many different writing styles. It has proven to be surprisingly adaptable to new ways of telling the same old stories, and there has been a trend in recent years for rewriting the Bible for niche readerships. Same message, new words.

A GLASGOW BIBLE

Written in colourful Glasgow vernacular, this collection of Auld and New Testament stories by Jamie Stuart breathes new life into familiar tales.

'There wis a gey rich man livin in the land o Uz. His name wis Job. Tae say that he wis rich is pittin in mildly, for he wis the maist well-heeled man in the hale land – a kina entrepeneur o his time. This man owned seven thoosan sheep, three thoosan camels, five hunner female donkeys. He had mony servants oan his pey-roll.'

THE COCKNEY BIBLE

'This Jesus geezer, God's currant bun, really does love us all,' says the Introduction to this adaptation of the Bible into cockney rhyming slang. The author, Mike Coles, says the intention is to capture people's attention by bringing the Bible back down to earth.

'God then said to Noah, "OK, me ol' china. I want you to get into the nanny with all your family. You are the only geezer in the whole bloomin' world who does the right thing, that's why I'm saving you and your family. I want you to take seven pairs of each kind of ritually clean animal (that means they are clean animals in a religious sort of way), and one pair of each kind of animal that is not clean in a religious sort of way.'

THE MANGA BIBLE

A recent publication, by talented Christian illustrator Siku, adapts the Bible into the visual language of Japanese Manga comic strip. Created for the younger, anime-literate generation, this is an edgy, provocative telling of the Bible, but always faithful to the text.

THE OUTDOOR BIBLE

'The water slid right off, as did a little mud ... the Bible dried out completely within two hours ... I''ll give it a big hosanna,' says one enthusiastic endorser of this waterproof Bible in a review that poses more questions than it answers. Have a look for yourself, and be as messy as you please: www.theoutdoorbible.com.

THE LIMERICK BIBLE

The entire Bible story told over the course of several hundred limericks, by the writer Peter Wallis.

> *'St Matthew records how wise men*
> *Set out towards Jerusalem*
> *Though their info was good*
> *They just misunderstood*
> *That they should have been heading for Bethl'hem.*
>
> *The result? They were some two years late*
> *But their guiding star for them did not wait*
> *Such relief when they saw it*
> *They could not ignore it*
> *For it led to the child pure and great.'*

THE KLINGON BIBLE

buy' ngop The US-based Klingon Language Institute is developing an entire Bible translated into the Klingon tongue. They have already translated and published a Klingon translation of Shakespeare's *Hamlet*, so this is not as unlikely a project as it sounds.

THE BOOK OF CEILING CAT

Almost, but not quite, as bizarre is an adaptation of the Bible in 'Kitty Pidgin', a hugely popular, idiosyncratic dialect developed by internet users, which juxtaposes photographs of cats with grammar-lite text. The Bible, which refers to God as 'Ceiling Cat', is likely to irritate those not in the loop but one can't deny that it is an original, innovative project taking the Bible to a new audience. Here is Psalm 23 ('The Lord is my shepherd'), Lolcat-style:

'Ceiling Cat iz mai sheprd. He givz me evrithin I need.
He letz me sleeps in teh sunni spot an haz liek nice waterz r ovar thar.
He makez mai soul happi an maeks sure I go teh riet wai for him. Liek
    thru teh cat flap insted of out teh opin windo LOL.
I iz in teh valli of dogz, fearin no pooch, bcz Ceiling Cat iz besied me rub-
    bin' mah ears, an it maek me so kumfy.'

THE TINY BIBLE

Three scientists from MIT (Massachusetts Institute of Technolo-
gy) created the world's smallest ever printed book in 2001 – the
entire New Testament on a tablet 5mm square. Every letter is the
size of a red blood cell or a small bacterium.

THE ANAGRAMMED BIBLE

This curious book by Richard Brodie and Mike Keith takes three
complete books of the Old Testament – the wisdom books of
Proverbs, Ecclesiastes and Song of Songs – and reorders the letters of each verse into an anagram. So, Proverbs 26:21, 'As coals are
to burning coals, and wood to fire; so is a contentious man to kindle
strife' becomes: 'Alas, son: words too unkind, or mean acts, can soon
ignite atrocious battlefields of ire.'

THE BLOKE'S BIBLE

A powerful, hard-bitten book of stories adapted from and inspired
by the Bible written and packaged in a style for men to feel comfortable reading in the pub. The author, Dave Hopwood, says in his
Introduction: 'I hope it makes you laugh, cry, get angry and get
quiet. Perhaps all in the space of time it takes to drink a pint.'

'Jesus pushes the hair from his eyes and spits in the sand. There are
streaks of mud on his fingers. Behind him, in the distance, a blind girl
is still wiping the muck from her face. Only she's not blind any more,
and she'll take that muck home and treasure it forever.'

*'Christianity is not a theory or
speculation, but a life; not a philosophy
of life, but a living presence.'*

SAMUEL TAYLOR COLERIDGE

❋{ BaD GUYS OF THE BIBLE }❋

Mwahahahaha! *Enter and gaze upon this gallery of rogues ... if you dare!*

CAIN

In addition to being the first person ever to be born
of natural childbirth (and presumably bearer of the world's
first ever navel?), Cain was humankind's first ever
murderer, slaying his younger brother Abel in a field.

✣

PHARAOH

There have been many pharaohs – kings of Egypt –
but the most infamous in biblical history was probably
Ahmose I, founder of the 18th Dynasty. This was the king
who enslaved the Israelites and ordered the death of every
newborn Hebrew boy. He was eventually challenged by
Moses and his plague-bringing staff.

✣

GOLIATH

The Philistine army's one-man war machine,
Goliath stood over nine feet tall and struck terror into
the hearts of the Israelite army. 'Give me one man
and let us fight each other!' he bellowed. Step forward
David, with a sling and a stone.

✣

SAUL

Once the King of Israel, Saul lost God's favour and,
possessed by an evil spirit, his life spiralled into
bitterness and jealousy of Israel's new young hero, David.
The rivalry between the two, complicated by Saul's son
Jonathan's friendship with David, against the backdrop of
the ongoing war between Israel and the Philistines,
is one of the great Bible narratives. Saul eventually
fell on his own sword after defeat in battle.

✣

JEZEBEL

As wife of King Ahab, Jezebel brought worship of the deity
Baal into Israel, and was believed to be the power behind
an increasingly despotic and murderous throne.

✣

NEBUCHADNEZZAR

Called the 'destroyer of nations' by the prophet
Jeremiah, this King of Babylon holds particular
significance among biblical bad guys. He was the first
of Israel's enemies to capture Jerusalem
where, under his command, Babylonians destroyed
the Temple and looted the bronze, silver and gold
therein. It is worth noting that the Israelite leaders
themselves were hardly blameless at this low point in
the nation's history. At the time of Nebuchadnezzar's
victory, Zedekiah was King of Judah and, like many of
his predecessors, including Ahab, Manasseh and
Jehoiakim, 'did evil in the eyes of the Lord'.

✣

HEROD

Vilified in thousands of nativity plays around
the world, King Herod the Great is the original biblical
baddie for most children today – he is the Guy Fawkes of
Christmas. A non-Jew, Herod was the Roman-appointed
King of Judea at the time of Jesus' birth and, terrified by
the supposed Messiah's arrival, ordered the death of every
boy aged two and under in Bethlehem.

✤

JUDAS

The disciple who betrayed Jesus by leading the Jewish
authorities to him at the Mount of Olives. He was paid thirty
silver coins for the deed, although some argue that his
motivation was not money but a desire to force a military
revolt against the Romans, with Jesus as the figurehead.
Whatever the reason, he fulfilled Jesus' earlier prediction
that he would be the one to expose him, and the name
Judas has become synonymous with betrayal.

✤

SAUL OF TARSUS

Before his dramatic Damascus Road conversion the
apostle Paul was Saul of Tarsus, prominent Pharisee and
scourge of the early ehurch. We first meet him in the book
of Acts as an approving bystander at the savage murder of
Stephen – an event which marked the outbreak of horrific
persecution of Christians, spearheaded by the man who
would later become one of the greatest apostles.

✤

SIMON THE MAGICIAN

Simon, the charismatic sorcerer of Samaria, is
mentioned relatively briefly in the Bible, converting
to Christ and joining the ministry of the apostles Philip,
John and Peter before being discredited by Peter for
offering to pay for gifts of the Holy Spirit (from which story
the term *simony* is derived). However, Simon's infamy
spreads beyond the pages of the Bible; he was one of the
most influential figures in the 1st and 2nd-century
Gnostic movement, painted by the Church Fathers as
the quintessential apostle of heresy. One legend
states that Simon met his end in a mighty showdown
of magic and miracles with Peter, now the first Pope,
in Rome. Simon attempted to fly from the top of the
Roman Forum, but instead fell to his death.

⁂{ LEGENDS OF ANGELS }⁂

Here follow ten Christian beliefs about angels.

- Angels are beings that are *intermediate* between God and humanity.

- There is an *innumerable* multitude of angels.

- Angels comprise the *heavenly court* of God, eternally singing praises to him.

- The medieval theologian Dionysius established a classification system for angels in his book *The Celestial Hierarchy*. They reside in three tiers, or spheres, of heaven.

  First sphere (closest to the throne of God): Cherubim, Seraphim, Ophanim.

  Second sphere (governors of heaven): Thrones, Dominions, Principalities.

  Third sphere (messengers and soldiers): Powers, Archangels, Angels. Angels are those most likely to interact with us here on earth.

- Angels are not to be confused with human souls. Some theologians have described them as intelligences never destined to be united with a body, thus making them *immortal and incorruptible* (although the Bible also speaks of fallen angels).

- Theologians have differed over when angels were *created*. Some believe it was at the same time as the heavens. Others that they were created at the same time as the material universe, or the same time as light, at which point all angels were tested and committed either to supernatural blessing (good angels) or eternal damnation (bad, or fallen angels).

- Sometimes angels are charged with particular *missions* to men and women.

- Angels have and will *attend Jesus*. They accompanied him during his temptation in the wilderness. An angel opened the tomb after Jesus' resurrection. Jesus himself says that his Second Coming will be accompanied by all the angels.

- Three good archangels are *named* in the Bible: Michael, 'the great prince who protects the people of God'; Gabriel, who appeared to Zechariah and Mary to foretell the births of John the Baptist and Jesus; and Raphael, who appears in human form to accompany Tobias (Raphael is only named in the deuterocanonical book of Tobit).

- *Fallen angels* are angels that have been banished from heaven for disobeying or rebelling against God. Satan is the most celebrated fallen angel. The book of Genesis also tells us of the Nephilim, a race of giants spawned by fallen angels interbreeding with human women.

✳{ curious church names }✳

A list of uniquely dedicated British churches.

ST ADELINE, Little Sudbury, Gloucestershire

✣

THE BEHEADING OF ST JOHN THE BAPTIST. Included for curiosity's sake but not actually unique – this is the dedication of two churches: Doddington in Kent and Westbourne in Sussex.

✣

ST BENEDICT BISCOP, Wombourne, Staffordshire

✣

ST DINABO, Llandinabo, Herefordshire

✣

ST EGELWINE-THE-MARTYR, Scalford, Leicestershire

✣

ST ESPRIT, Marton, Warwickshire

✣

ST FABIAN AND ST SEBASTIAN, Woodbastwick, Norfolk

✣

ST KYNEBURGA, Castor, Cambridgeshire

✣

ST PROTASE AND ST GERVASE, Little Plumstead, Norfolk

✣

ST WANDREGESELIUS, Bixley, Norfolk

✲⟨ Ten Descriptions of Heaven ⟩✲

The Bible contains many descriptions of heaven, some metaphorical like Jesus' parables, and others prophetic visions that many Christians believe to be literal.

ENTRY TO HEAVEN

Jesus tried to explain who would enter the kingdom of heaven to his disciples in a number of parables. Heaven is like a net full of fish – angels will separate the righteous from the unrighteous, like fishermen sorting their catch at the end of the day (Matthew 13:47–50). Similarly, it is like a king's wedding banquet – many will be invited but refuse to attend; they will be thrown into the darkness while others take their place (Matthew 22:1–14).

MANY ROOMS

Jesus described heaven as a house with many rooms, to which he would go in advance to prepare a place for his disciples (John 14:2–3).

REUNITED

In heaven we will be reunited both with Jesus and with those believers who have died and gone before us (1 Thessalonians 4:13–17).

IMPERISHABLE BODIES

Flesh and blood will not inherit heaven but we will all be changed into something imperishable (1 Corinthians 15:50, 54).

ANGELS

There are huge numbers of angels in heaven – 'thousands upon thousands, and ten thousand times ten thousand' – and we will join them and all other creatures singing praises to God (Revelation 5:11–13).

SERVING GOD

A great multitude, from all nations, will stand in white robes before the throne of God, and will serve him all day and all night (Revelation 7:9–17).

A HOLY CITY

There will be a mighty city in heaven, the New Jerusalem. It will be the shape of a perfect cube, and its walls made of precious materials such as gold and jasper, inlaid with precious stones. Its gates will be made of pearl, and its streets of pure gold, like transparent glass (Revelation 21).

RIVER OF LIFE

The river of life, bordered by the fruit-growing tree of life, will flow through the city (Revelation 22:1–2).

LIGHT

There will be no more night, and no need for lamps or the light of the sun (Revelation 22:5).

AN END TO DEATH

There will be no more death or mourning or crying or pain (Revelation 21:4).

❧ THE JOY OF SONG ❧

In the Song of Songs, the Bible showcases a beautiful, intimate love poem believed to have been written by King Solomon. This abridgement gives us a taste but hardly does justice to the subtle, sensual, erotic power of the whole, which is written as a dialogue between a man (Lover) and woman (Beloved).

Beloved:
'Let him kiss me with the kisses of his mouth –
for your love is more delightful than wine.'

Lover:
'How beautiful you are, my darling!
Oh, how beautiful!
Your eyes are like doves.'

Beloved:
'Like an apple tree among the trees of the forest
is my lover among the young men.
I delight to sit in his shade,
and his fruit is sweet to my taste.'

Lover:
'Your lips are like a scarlet ribbon;
your mouth is lovely.
Your temples behind your veil
are like the halves of a pomegranate.
Your neck is like the tower of David,
built with elegance;
on it hang a thousand shields,
all of them shields of warriors.
Your two breasts are like two fawns,
like twin fawns of a gazelle

that browse among the lilies.
Until the day breaks
and the shadows flee,
I will go to the mountain of myrrh
and to the hill of incense.'

Beloved:
'Awake, north wind,
and come, south wind!
Blow on my garden,
that its fragrance may spread abroad.
Let my lover come into his garden
and taste its choice fruits.'

Lover:
'I have come into my garden, my sister, my bride;
I have gathered my myrrh with my spice.
I have eaten my honeycomb and my honey;
I have drunk my wine and my milk.'

Beloved:
'My lover thrust his hand through the latch-opening;
my heart began to pound for him.
I arose to open for my lover,
and my hands dripped with myrrh,
my fingers with flowing myrrh,
on the handles of the lock.'

Lover:
'Your stature is like that of the palm,
and your breasts like clusters of fruit.
I said, "I will climb the palm tree;
I will take hold of its fruit."
May your breasts be like the clusters of the vine,

the fragrance of your breath like apples,
and your mouth like the best wine.'

Beloved:
'May the wine go straight to my lover,
flowing gently over lips and teeth.
I belong to my lover,
and his desire is for me.'

'Let us go early to the vineyards
to see if the vines have budded,
if their blossoms have opened,
and if the pomegranates are in bloom –
there I will give you my love.'

'Under the apple tree I roused you;
there your mother conceived you,
there she who was in labour gave you birth.
Place me like a seal over your heart,
like a seal on your arm;
for love is as strong as death,
its jealousy unyielding as the grave.
It burns like blazing fire,
like a mighty flame.
Many waters cannot quench love;
rivers cannot wash it away.'

'Come away, my lover,
and be like a gazelle
or like a mighty stag
on the spice-laden mountains.'

✢⟩ THE Year's Journey ⟨✢

Christians use the church calendar to chart and structure their spiritual journey and devotion over the course of a year. The sequence of seasons and festivals modelled on the life and ministry of Jesus helps us to reflect on the particular challenges and blessings of the Christian faith.

ADVENT

The start of the Christian year, the period of Advent – meaning 'coming' – begins on the fourth Sunday before Christmas Day. Remembering Jesus' coming at Christmas, Christians use this time to focus also on the meaning of his Second Coming at the end of the age.

CHRISTMAS AND EPIPHANY

The Twelve Days of Christmas, starting on 24 December, celebrate the birth of Jesus and include, on 6 January, Epiphany – the day on which we remember the visit of the Magi to the newborn Jesus in Bethlehem. Epiphany – meaning 'revealing' – reminds us that Jesus was born as Saviour to the whole world, Jews and Gentiles alike.

LENT

The period of forty days preceding Easter is known as Lent. Beginning with Ash Wednesday, it marks the time Jesus spent in the wilderness following his baptism. Christians observe his temptation by considering the disciplines of faith, and often choose to 'give up' a worldly pleasure during this time.

HOLY WEEK

At the end of Lent comes Holy Week, which
mirrors the events of the Passion of Jesus – from his final
triumphal entry to Jerusalem, through the Last Supper, his
betrayal, trial and crucifixion.

EASTER

The major festival of the Christian year,
celebrating the resurrection of Jesus from the dead
and the final victory over death for us all.

ASCENSION DAY

This celebration, always on a Thursday, takes
place forty days after Easter Sunday and marks Jesus'
ascension into heaven after the post-resurrection days
spent among his disciples.

PENTECOST AND TRINITY SUNDAY

Marking the end of the first, festival-heavy half
of the church year, Pentecost takes place fifty days after
Easter and remembers the anointing of the Holy Spirit on
the apostles and disciples to give them power to minister
the good news of Jesus to the world. Trinity Sunday, one
week later, focuses on the three-personed nature
of God and sums up all the observances of the
Advent to Pentecost period.

ORDINARY TIME

The second half of the church year is
known as Ordinary Time, from 'ordinal' meaning
'counted time'. During this season leading up to
Advent, Christians focus on various aspects
of faith, particularly the mission of the
Church to the world.

*'Amazing grace! How sweet the sound
That saved a wretch like me!'*

JOHN NEWTON

⁎⟨ LIVES OF THE CELTIC SAINTS ⟩⁎

Adventurous and world-loving, passionate and holy, the saints of the Celtic Church brought light and hope to the violent, confused world of the Dark Ages. These astonishing men and women renounced all material comforts in their mission to spread the gospel across pagan Britain and Europe, yet their lives were rich in character and miracles. Such is their legend it is difficult to separate the facts from the myths but this hardly seems to matter, so positive has their influence been.

ST MARTIN (C.316–97)

The saint: Renowned for *living* the gospel rather than merely preaching it.

The history: A Roman officer who refused to fight once he converted to Christianity. Became Bishop of Tours, France, and later lived the life of a hermit.

The legend: Cut his officer's cloak and gave half of it to a beggar. He later had a vision of Jesus wearing the half he had given away. Patron saint of geese.

ST NINIAN (C.360–432)

The saint: Passionate and zealous for perfection in all aspects of faith.

The history: Born in Galloway, he left to train for the clergy and eventually become a bishop in Rome, before returning to bring his faith to the Britons and Picts of Scotland. Established *Candida Casa* in Whithorn, the first ever church and Christian community north of Hadrian's Wall.

The legend: One night, he protected the livestock of his farmers with an invisible holy circle. Next morning, he discovered thieves had broken into the circle but, unable to escape, their leader had been killed by a bull. In grief, Ninian prayed for the thief, who was miraculously brought back to life.

ST PATRICK (387–493)

The saint: Defiant and pioneering, the father of Christianity in Ireland.

The history: Born in Britain, to a Roman family, he was kidnapped by Irish marauders at the age of sixteen and was a shepherd slave in the north of Ireland for the next six years. He later returned to evangelise Ireland and gained tolerance and organisation for the scattered Christian communities in the pagan country.

The legend: Banished all snakes from Ireland (some believe the snakes to be symbolic of the druids).

ST DAVID (C.520–C.600)

The saint: A great preacher, contemplative and extremely strict ascetic.

The history: Believed to have been born to a noble family, he founded twelve monasteries in Wales, Cornwall and Brittany. Summoned the so-called 'Synod of Victory' at Caerleon in Wales which finally defeated the Pelagian heresy (denial of the concept of original sin) in Britain.

The legend: When preaching to a crowd so large that some could not see him, the ground on which he stood rose up to form a small hill.

ST BRENDAN (C.484–C.577)

The saint: An eccentric adventurer who believed he might one day discover heaven on earth.

The history: A travelling ordained monk, he founded many monasteries in Ireland and Scotland. Also known as 'Brendan the Voyager'.

The legend: The *Navigation of St Brendan* was published in the 10th century, telling of the saint's many years spent sailing the Atlantic in a small leather coracle. At one point he found a small island that turned out to be the back of a living whale; Brendan often returned to the whale and celebrated Easter upon its back.

ST KENTIGERN (C.518–603)

The saint: Also known as St Mungo, his compassionate and cheerful demeanour attracted the hearts of all who beheld him.

The history: Grandson of a British prince, he was born and raised in Scotland. Preached to the Britons around Strathclyde, but when persecuted took his ministry to Cumbria and Wales before returning to the Glasgow area.

The legend: As a young man, Kentigern brought back to life the pet robin of his master St Serf, after his fellow students accidentally killed it in a game.

ST COLUMBA (C.521–97)

The saint: Statesman, abbot, missionary and elegant preacher, Columba would rarely rest. Behind closed doors his time was spent in prayer, study and writing.

The history: Perhaps the greatest of missionaries to Scotland and Northumbria. Columba was born to an Irish noble family and, after becoming a priest, founded several monasteries in Ireland. Later founded a monastery on the island of Iona, from which base he and his twelve companions evangelised the mainland and neighbouring islands.

The legend: When refused admittance to the residence of Brude, King of the Picts, Columba made the sign of the cross over the locked gates and the bolts flew open. The miracle led to Brude's conversion.

ST COLUMBAN (C.550—615)

The saint: Restless, passionate and headstrong, and zealous for the tradition of his Celtic forefathers.

The history: A native of Ireland, he travelled and established several monasteries in France and Italy, spreading his own Celtic-inspired monastic rule into mainland Europe.

The legend: Destroyed with a single breath a large cauldron of beer which pagans intended as a sacrifice to their god Wodan.

ST CUTHBERT (634—87)

The saint: Fair, strong and of a ruddy countenance, he had the human touch and was widely admired.

The history: As Prior and then Bishop of Lindisfarne, he oversaw implementation of the Roman liturgy and also a period of great missionary zeal and energy. Because of the Viking invasions it was more than 300 years before Cuthbert's body was finally laid to rest in peace at Durham Cathedral.

The legend: Once a shepherd, he had a vision one night of the Irish monk St Aidan being carried to heaven by angels and this prompted Cuthbert to become a monk himself.

ST BRIGID (C.451—C.523)

The saint: Practical and wise, high-spirited and eternally generous.

The history: The daughter of a noble father and slave mother, Brigid was sold to a druid whom she later converted. Founded the first convent in Ireland at Kildare, and was influential in the growth of the early Irish Church

The legend: Perhaps remembered best of all for her generosity – feeding the half-starved hound or giving the king's sword to a passing beggar.

✺꜏ CHRISTIAN SYMBOLS ꜏✺

A common symbol for God, *Alpha* and *Omega* are the first and last letters of the Greek alphabet. 'I am the Alpha and the Omega,' says God in the book of Revelation. He is eternal, the beginning and the end of time.

Replacing the full Hebrew name for God, *Yahweh*, which according to Jewish tradition is too sacred to be written or spoken aloud.

An equilateral triangle represents God as the three-personed Trinity. God the Father, God the Son and God the Holy Spirit are as equal as the three sides and angles of this triangle.

Most commonly associated with Judaism today, but this six-pointed star also appears in Christian symbolism with a particular reference to the Creation (at which God as Trinity was present – the two interlaced triangles demonstrate his eternal nature).

The fish is a secret symbol for Jesus used by 1st-century believers. Its key is the Greek word for fish, *Ichthus*, also an acronym for the Greek phrase *Iesous Christos Theou Huios Soter* (Jesus Christ, Son of God, Saviour).

Christian images of a dove generally symbolise the Holy Spirit, the form in which he appeared in bodily form and descended upon Jesus at his baptism.

This symbol, known as Chi Rho, combines the first two letters of the Greek word for Christ, *Xpictoc*. It was popularised as a Christian symbol when Constantine, the first Christian Roman Emperor, used it on his banners.

The empty cross is possibly the most powerful of Christian symbols, demonstrating Jesus' victory over death and the opportunity of new life for us all.

 A less familiar representation of the cross, possibly reflecting the proper shape of the crucifixion cross.

The cross with a circle around its cross-section originates from Celtic regions of Ireland and Great Britain, although the exact meaning of the circle has never been determined.

 The cross is sometimes represented with an additional, small crossbar near the top, representing the plaque attached to the cross above Jesus' head which the Bible tells us read 'This is Jesus, King of the Jews'. This symbol is known as the Patriarchal Cross.

A variation on the Patriarchal Cross, with a third, slanted crossbar near the base, representing the wood to which Jesus' feet were nailed. This symbol is known as the Eastern Orthodox Cross.

 The Papal Cross, which has three high crossbars, was traditionally the shape of the Pope's pastoral staff. Although he now carries a single-barred cross, it remains a symbol of the papal office.

✳⟨ DEATHS OF THE APOSTLES ⟩✳

So strong was their faith in Jesus that an estimated 70 million peo-
ple have died in his name, many for refusing to deny his divinity
and Messiahship. Each of the apostles — those who knew Jesus best
of all — was prepared to face a gruesome death for his sake. Only
three of the accounts below are recorded in the Bible, and so consid-
ered canonical; the others stem from less reliable documents and
oral traditions.

ANDREW

Crucified in Greece. Tradition has it that Andrew
was originally bound to a cross in the same shape as that of
Jesus but, at his own request as he believed himself unwor-
thy, he was taken down and placed instead on an X-shaped
cross. He continued to preach to his torturers from the
cross for two days before he eventually died.

✥

BARTHOLOMEW

Flayed alive with a whip and then crucified upside
down, in Armenia. See also under Philip.

✥

JAMES (SON OF ZEBEDEE)

Beheaded in Judea. King Herod ordered James's death by
the sword. Legend says his body was taken by angels and
sailed in a rudderless, unattended boat to Spain, where a
massive rock closed around it.

✥

JAMES (SON OF ALPHAEUS)

Crucified in Egypt.

✠

JOHN

Died peacefully in Turkey. He is the only one of
the apostles believed to have avoided martyrdom, although
the phrase 'there but for the grace of God go I' would have
been apt for John. He was boiled in a barrel of burning oil
in front of a packed Colosseum in Rome but emerged
unharmed, prompting the conversion of thousands
who had witnessed the miracle.

✠

JUDAS

Took his own life in Judea. The Bible
carries two different accounts of Judas's death. Matthew
reports that he hanged himself after remorsefully returning his thirty pieces of silver to the chief priests and elders.
The book of Acts claims he spent the money on a field
where he subsequently fell over, his body bursting open
and intestines spilling out. One attempt to reconcile these
accounts suggests that the priests used the money to buy
the field in which stood the tree from which he hanged
himself. When his dead body finally fell, it was decom-
posed and so broke open on the ground.

✠

JUDE

Martyred in Persia. Possibly with Simon the Zealot.

✠

MATTHEW

Martyred by the sword in Ethiopia.

✠

MATTHIAS

Stoned and beheaded, or crucified, in Armenia.

✠

PHILIP

Crucified upside down in Turkey. His
fellow apostle Bartholomew was reportedly crucified
alongside him, but released by the onlookers before he
died because of the power of Philip's preaching. Philip
himself refused to be released, and died.

✠

SIMON PETER

Crucified upside down in Rome. It is said that he asked to
be nailed to the cross upside down so that he would not be
considered an equal of Jesus.

✠

SIMON THE ZEALOT

Martyred in Persia. Possibly with fellow apostle Jude,
although there are other stories of Simon's death. One tradition says he was crucified while another claims he was
sawn in half. The place of his death is also disputed, with
various claims that he met his end in Samaria, Caucasian
Iberia and even Lincolnshire in Britain.

✠

THOMAS

Martyred in India. It has been recorded that Thomas was impaled with a spear in India, where he was the first to take the gospel.

✢

The deaths of a few other significant contemporaries and followers of Jesus.

✢

JOHN THE BAPTIST

Beheaded in Judea. John was imprisoned by Herod Antipas for speaking out against the ruler's adulterous relationship with Herodias, his brother's wife. At the request of Salome, daughter of Herodias, the prophet's head was chopped off and presented to her on a plate.

✢

JAMES (BROTHER OF JESUS)

Martyred in Jerusalem. This leader of the first church in Jerusalem, who has been called 'the Lord's brother', was killed by the Jewish authorities. Some say he was stoned to death, while others say he was thrown from the roof of the Temple and then beaten to death with a club.

✢

PAUL

Beheaded in Rome. Possibly the most influential human in the history of the Church, Paul eventually met his end at the command of the Emperor Nero. One legend has it that he was beheaded on the left bank of the Tiber and three fountains sprang forth where his head bounced three times.

⁕⟩ PLANTS OF THE BIBLE ⟨⁕

THE GARDEN OF EDEN

A highlight of God's original creation plan
was a beautiful garden he planted in the east, where
Adam was placed to live. All kinds of trees grew in the
garden, 'trees that were pleasing to the eye and good
for food', and the centrepieces were the tree of life
and the tree of the knowledge of good and evil
(Adam was ordered not to eat from the latter).

BULRUSH

The three-month-old baby Moses was placed in a small
basket made of bulrushes (or papyrus) and hidden in the
reeds along the banks of the Nile to escape the Pharaoh's
horrific cull of newborn Israelite boys.

BURNING BUSH

Later in life, having fled Egypt, Moses was
tending sheep when God spoke to him from within a bush
that was on fire but did not burn up. It was here that Moses
received the command to liberate his people and lead them
out of Egypt to the Promised Land.

MANDRAKE

'You must sleep with me. I have hired you with my son's
mandrakes.' One of the Bible's most eye-opening lines of
dialogue. Jealous sisters Leah and Rachel were competing
for the attentions of their shared husband Jacob. When
Leah's son Reuben found some mandrake plants (a 'love
plant' believed to have magical fertility powers), she traded
them with Rachel for a night with Jacob, with whom she

had been out of favour. She conceived and named her new
son Issachar, a pun on the Hebrew word for 'hired'.

OAK

It is believed that 'the great tree of Moreh' at
Shechem, where God told Abraham he would give the land
to his descendants, was a mighty oak. Hundreds of years
later the Israelites, now under the leadership of Joshua,
renewed their promises and commitment to God at this
same oak. Joshua placed a large stone under the tree as a
mark of the renewed covenant.

OLIVE TREES

The olive tree is still today a notable feature
of Palestine, where it was cultivated long before
Hebrew times. It is mentioned many times in the Bible.
Noah's dove brought him an olive branch to show God's
mercy. A talking olive tree was used in a parable by Jotham,
in protest at the coronation of Abimelech. Jesus and his
disciples spent a lot of time at the Mount of Olives, from
where he eventually ascended to heaven. Paul uses
ingrafted wild olive branches to illustrate the
notion of salvation coming to the Gentiles.

LILIES

Another frequently mentioned biblical plant,
although it is not always clear which species is being
referred to. Lilies are used on a number of occasions
in the love poetry of the Song of Songs ('Like a lily
among thorns is my darling among the maidens'),
and Jesus talks of the 'lilies of the field' when he tells
us not to worry about what we wear.

PALMS

When Jesus arrived at Jerusalem for the
Passover feast shortly before his betrayal, ecstatic crowds
greeted him as the Messiah, waving palm branches as he
rode into the city on a donkey.

JERUSALEM THORN

Some believe that the crown of thorns placed on Jesus'
head before his crucifixion was made of the spiky branches
of the small *paliurus spina-christi* tree, also known as
'Jerusalem thorn' or 'Christ's thorn'.

WORMWOOD

Wormwood is a herb of bitter taste mentioned
on several occasions in the Bible. Most notably it is the
name given to the star that falls to earth, making the waters
poisonous and undrinkable, in John's Revelation prophecy. Some believe this meant the waters became overgrown
with wormwood. Wormwood is also the name of C. S.
Lewis's novice devil in his book *The Screwtape Letters*.

✦ THE WISDOM OF JESUS ✦

A selection of the most popular sayings of Jesus.

'The time has come. The kingdom of God is near. Repent and believe the good news!' (Mark 1:15)

...

'It is easier for a camel to go through the eye of a needle than for a rich man to enter the kingdom of God'. (Mark 10:25)

...

'Many who are first will be last, and the last first'. (Mark 10:31)

...

'Blessed are the poor in spirit, for theirs is the kingdom of heaven.
Blessed are those who mourn, for they will be comforted.
Blessed are the meek, for they will inherit the earth.
Blessed are those who hunger and thirst for righteousness, for they will be filled.
Blessed are the merciful, for they will be shown mercy.
Blessed are the pure in heart, for they will see God.
Blessed are the peacemakers, for they will be called sons of God.
Blessed are those who are persecuted because of righteousness, for theirs is the kingdom of heaven.'
(Matthew 5:3–10)

...

'If someone strikes you on the right cheek, turn to him the other one also'. (Matthew 5:39)

...

'This, then, is how you should pray:

> "Our Father in heaven,
> hallowed be your name,
> your kingdom come,
> your will be done
> on earth as it is in heaven.
> Give us today our daily bread.
> Forgive us our debts,
> as we also have forgiven our debtors.
> And lead us not into temptation,
> but deliver us from the evil one."'
> (Matthew 6:9–13)

•••

'Come, follow me, and I will make you fishers of men'. (Matthew 4:19)

•••

'For God so loved the world that he gave his one and only Son, that whoever believes in him shall not perish but have eternal life'. (John 3:16)

•••

'I am the light of the world. Whoever follows me will never walk in darkness, but will have the light of life'. (John 8:12)

•••

'It is written "My house will be a house of prayer" but you have made it "a den of robbers"'. (Luke 19:46)

•••

The seven sayings of Jesus on the cross are often grouped together as a devotional meditation for use in Holy Week:

'Father, forgive them, for they do not know what they are doing.'
'I tell you the truth, today you will be with me in paradise.'
'Dear woman, here is your son; here is your mother.'
'Eloi, Eloi, lama sabachthani?' ('My God, my God, why have you forsaken me?')
'I am thirsty.'
'It is finished.'
'Father, into your hands I commit my spirit.'
(From Matthew 27, Luke 23 and John 19)

'The Bible tells us to love our neighbours, and also to love our enemies; probably because they are generally the same people.'

G. K. CHESTERTON

❊ controversial verse ❊

A small number of hymns that sound comfortingly familiar to us now but have not always been so inoffensive.

GOD SAVE OUR GRACIOUS QUEEN

The British national anthem is thought to date back to 1688 but its fervently nationalist tone makes it sit rather uncomfortably in hymn books. *Hymns Ancient and Modern* substituted the second verse (including the lines 'Scatter her enemies, and make them fall') with a less provocative version in 1836.

✣

O, FOR A THOUSAND TONGUES TO SING

This popular Methodist hymn by Charles Wesley (1739) has several problematic lines, including Jesus breaking 'the power of cancelled sin' (see note on Wesley under 'Most Popular Hymns') and 'wash the Ethiop white'. It is generally sung today with some verses omitted.

✣

LOVE DIVINE, ALL LOVES EXCELLING

Another theologically contentious Charles Wesley (1747) hymn. See the entry for this hymn in 'Most Popular Hymns'.

✣

AND DID THOSE FEET IN ANCIENT TIMES

William Blake wrote these verses in 1804, but there was some question over whether it qualified as a hymn. It made its first appearance in a hymn book in 1923, complete with the famous *Jerusalem* tune by Herbert Parry.

BRIGHTEST AND BEST OF THE SONS OF THE MORNING

It took a while for this hymn by Reginald Heber to be accepted as such, possibly because of concern that it seemed to advocate worship of a star. It was finally printed in a hymn book in 1827, a year after Heber tragically drowned in a swimming pool.

✢

NEARER, MY GOD, TO THEE

It took a long time for this 1841 hymn by Sarah Adams to be accepted by Christians. Accordant with Adams's Unitarian beliefs, it does not mention the divinity of Jesus.

✢

CITY OF GOD, HOW BROAD AND FAR

Another Unitarian writer, Samuel Johnson, penned this one in 1860 but, with no mention of Jesus or the Holy Spirit, it took until 1950 before it first appeared in a Christian hymn book, *Hymns Ancient and Modern*.

✢

FOR THE BEAUTY OF THE EARTH

Folliott Sandford Pierpoint wrote this one in 1863. *Hymns Ancient and Modern* changed several lines and dropped three verses from the original which, with such references as 'our sacrifice of praise', 'the Martyrs' crown of light' and 'thy Virgin's robes of snow', were considered too Catholic for the Anglican hymnal.

✢

ONWARD, CHRISTIAN SOLDIERS

The militant language of triumphalist Christianity in this hymn is not as palatable today as it may have been when written by Sabine Baring-Gould in 1864, and it is no longer included in many hymn books.

✢

O VALIANT HEARTS, WHO TO YOUR GLORY CAME

This was written by Sir John Arkwright in 1917, at the height of the First World War, and was popular in the first half of the last century but most hymn books now omit it, concerned that it glorifies war.

'A religion that is small enough for our understanding is not great enough for our need.'

ARTHUR JAMES BALFOUR

⁕{ IT came UPON A MIDNIGHT CLear ... }⁕

... Well, actually the time of Jesus' birth was never recorded. And now for a scrooge-ish debunking of other cherished nativity beliefs. Bah, humbug!

THE ANGEL GABRIEL APPEARED TO MARY AND JOSEPH

Gabriel appeared to Mary, as told in the Gospel
of Matthew, but we are only told that 'an angel' appeared
to Joseph in the Gospel of Luke, and there is no
evidence that it was Gabriel.

♣

A DONKEY CARRIED MARY FROM NAZARETH TO BETHLEHEM

The donkey is not mentioned in any of the Gospels.
She may have walked!

♣

THREE KINGS ...

They were actually wise men, or Magi –
possibly astrologers. The Bible does not mention
how many of them there were.

♣

... FOLLOWED THE STAR ...

Not all the way! Matthew records that the Magi
first spotted the star from their home in the East, but it did
not guide them from their homelands to Jerusalem – by far
the longest leg of their journey. It only guided them on the
short trip from Jerusalem to Bethlehem.

♣

... AND FOUND JESUS LYING IN A MANGER IN A STABLE

Jesus was in a house by the time the Magi arrived.

✣

HEROD WAS ALONE IN WORRYING ABOUT THE BIRTH OF JESUS

According to Matthew, the whole of Jerusalem was disturbed to hear the news of his birth.

✤ A journey for the soul ❧

Pilgrimage was an important aspect of Christian life in the Middle Ages for those that had the means to pursue it. Some would undertake the journey to a site of biblical significance or important saintly relic for a specific purpose – physical healing or to win indulgences to atone for sin – while for others it may have been for the rigorous spiritual test that would accompany the physical challenge. Many Christians, Roman Catholics in particular, still make pilgrimages today; there are many thousands of sites around the world, but here are ten of the most popular and fascinating.

BETHLEHEM, ISRAEL

The birthplace of Jesus. Pilgrims can visit the Church of the Nativity, built on the supposed site of his birth, and the Milk Grotto, where the Holy Family was said to have sheltered to escape Herod's wrath. In the latter, a scraping from the floor where Mary's milk is said to have spilled will apparently boost a woman's quantity of milk and fertility.

•••

CANTERBURY, ENGLAND

Britain's most famous pilgrimage site, Christians have been travelling to the shrine of the relics of St Thomas Becket, martyred Archbishop of Canterbury, since the 12th century. Geoffrey Chaucer's *Canterbury Tales*, written in the late 14th century, comprises the colourful tales recounted to one another by pilgrims on the Canterbury route.

•••

HEBRON, ISRAEL

The Cave of Machpelah, identified in the book of Genesis as the burial site of Abraham and Sarah.

•••

JERUSALEM, ISRAEL

In this most holy of cities, pilgrims can visit
the Church of the Holy Sepulchre, built on the site
of Jesus' crucifixion, burial and resurrection, the
Garden of Gethsemane at the foot of the Mount of Olives, a
building on Mount Zion said to be both the site of the
Last Supper and the tomb of King David, and the
Muslim Dome of the Rock shrine covering the
outcrop of Mount Moriah where some believe God
asked Abraham to sacrifice his young son Isaac.

•••

LOURDES, FRANCE

Several million pilgrims a year visit the town in
southwest France where the Virgin Mary appeared in a
series of visions to Bernadette Soubirous in 1958. Lourdes
is renowned as a site at which miraculous healings take
place, and its popularity is such that the town has a hotel
bed capacity second in the whole country only to Paris.

•••

MEDJUGORJE, BOSNIA AND HERZEGOVINA

An average of more than a million pilgrims a year
visit the village of Medjugorje where a group of children
had a series of visions of the Virgin Mary in 1981. Various
subsequent miracles, apparitions and prophecies have
surrounded both the site and some of the (now
grown-up) visionaries ever since.

•••

MOUNT CARMEL, ISRAEL

Christian pilgrims travel to pray at the fourteen
Stations of the Cross dedicated to Mary, and also to visit
the point on the mountain where Elijah's sacrifice was
consumed by heavenly fire.

MOUNT SINAI, EGYPT

St Catherine's Monastery marks the point where Moses saw the burning bush. A bush said to be grown from the same stock still grows there.

•••

SANTIAGO DE COMPOSTELA, SPAIN

This town was one of the three most important pilgrimage destinations for medieval Christians (alongside Jerusalem and Rome), and the 20th century saw a great revival of the tradition of hiking hundreds of miles over the French Pyrenees and across northern Spain to Compostela, home of the tomb of the apostle James.

•••

TAIZÉ, FRANCE

As many as 5000 pilgrims visit the Taizé community every week, attracted by the mystical strength of its communal, meditative prayer.

'Divine Scripture is the feast of wisdom, and the single books are the various dishes.'

St Ambrose

✳{ THE WORD OF DOG }✳

The Bible is the inerrant word of God ... or is it? Bible publishers are as human as the rest of us – I should know, I am one – and, while the demands for 100 per cent accuracy are perhaps greater than in any other field of publishing, the odd mistake will occasionally slip through. Here are ten mistakes that made it off the press, with the correct version in italics beneath.

THE BUG BIBLE (1551)

'Thou shalt not be afraid for the bugges by night'. (Psalm 91:5)

'Thou shalt not be afraid for the terror by night.'

··

THE PLACE-MAKERS' BIBLE (1562)

'Blessed are the place-makers: for they shall be called the children of God'. (Matthew 5:9)

'Blessed are the peacemakers: for they shall be called the children of God.'

··

THE TREACLE BIBLE (1568)

'Is there no treacle in Gilead?'. (Jeremiah 8:22)

'Is there no balm in Gilead?'

··

THE WICKED BIBLE (1631)

'Thou shalt commit adultery'. (Exodus 20:14)

'Thou shalt not commit adultery.'

··

THE UNRIGHTEOUS BIBLE (1653)

'Know ye not that the unrighteous shall inherit the
kingdom of God?'. (1 Corinthians 6:9)

*'Know ye not that the unrighteous shall not inherit
the kingdom of God?'*

··

THE PRINTERS' BIBLE (1702)

'Printers have persecuted me without a cause: but my heart
standeth in awe of thy word'. (Psalm 119:161)

*'Princes have persecuted me without a cause: but my heart standeth
in awe of thy word.'*

··

THE FIRST MURDERERS' BIBLE (1795)

'But Jesus said unto her, "Let the children first
be killed"'. (Mark 7:27)

'But Jesus said unto her, "Let the children first be filled."'

··

THE SECOND MURDERERS' BIBLE (1801)

'These are murderers, complainers,
walking after their own lusts'. (Jude 16)

'These are murmurers, complainers, walking after their own lusts.'

··

THE SMILING BIBLE (1810)

'He that hath ears to ear, let him hear'. (Matthew 11:15)

'He that hath ears to hear, let him hear.'

··

THE TEENAGERS' BIBLE (1964)

'I will ... that women adorn themselves in modern
apparel'. (1 Timothy 2:9)

'I will ... that women adorn themselves in modest apparel.'

I am grateful to biblical proofreaders extraordinaire, Peachtree Editorial Services of Atlanta, USA, for sending me the list above. They also showed me copies of a few typos in recent settings of the Bible which, to the likely relief of the publisher, they managed to spot before going to press:

'You have the message of eternal life, and we believe; we know that you ate the Holy One of God'. (John 6:69)

'You have the message of eternal life, and we believe; we know that you are the Holy One of God.'

..

'Felix was breaking the Jaw by continuing to detain Paul'. (footnote to Acts 24:27)

'Felix was breaking the law by continuing to detain Paul.'

..

'Meanwhile, as Simon Peter was standing by the fire warning himself, they asked him again'. (John 18:25)

'Meanwhile, as Simon Peter was standing by the fire warming himself, they asked him again.'

..

'Moses spent forty years in Pharaoh's court thinking he was somebody, forty years in the dessert learning he was a nobody'. (study note on Deuteronomy 34)

'Moses spent forty years in Pharaoh's court thinking he was some-body, forty years in the desert learning he was a nobody.'

..

'He who has the Son has a life; he who does not have the Son of God does not have a life'. (1 John 5:12)

'He who has the Son has life; he who does not have the Son of God does not have life.'

⊰ Ten Promises of God ⊱

The Bible is a source of comfort and encouragement to millions of Christians around the world. Through direct revelation, through prophecy and through the person of Jesus, God has made countless promises to those who believe and trust in him. Here are ten of the most significant.

MERCY

God (to Noah): 'I now establish my covenant
with you and with your descendants after you and every
living creature on earth. Never again will there be a flood to
destroy the earth. Whenever the rainbow appears in the
clouds, I will see it and remember the everlasting covenant
between God and all living creatures of every kind on
the earth'. (Genesis 9:9–16)

✛

SPIRITUAL INHERITANCE

God (to Abraham): 'I will make you into a great
nation and I will bless you; I will make your name great and
you will be a blessing. I will bless those who bless you and
whoever curses you I will curse; and all peoples on earth
will be blessed through you'. (Genesis 12:2–3)

✛

BLESSING FOR THE RIGHTEOUS

Jesus: 'Blessed are those who are persecuted
because of righteousness, for theirs is the kingdom of
heaven'. (Matthew 5:10)

PROTECTION

God: 'When you pass through the waters, I will be with you; and when you pass through the rivers, they will not sweep over you'. (Isaiah 43:2)

✚

STRENGTH AND COURAGE

God: 'Do not fear, for I am with you; do not be dismayed, for I am your God. I will strengthen you and help you; I will uphold you with my righteous right hand'. (Isaiah 41:10)

✚

REST

Jesus: 'Come to me, all you who are weary and burdened, and I will give you rest'. (Matthew 11:28)

✚

BLESSINGS

Jesus: 'Now is your time of grief, but I will see you again and you will rejoice, and no-one will take away your joy. In that day you will no longer ask me anything. I tell you the truth, my Father will give you whatever you ask in my name'. (John 16:22–3)

✚

SALVATION

Jesus: 'I am the resurrection and the life. He who believes in me will live, even though he dies; and whoever lives and believes in me will never die'. (John 11:25)

✚

A PLACE IN HEAVEN

Jesus: 'In my Father's house are many rooms. I am going there to prepare a place for you. And if I go and prepare a place for you, I will come back and take you to be with me that you may also be where I am'. (John 14:2–3)

✛

PEACE AND JUSTICE

God: 'The wolf and the lamb will feed together, and the lion will eat straw like the ox, but dust will be the serpent's food'. (Isaiah 65:25)

'The point of having an open mind, like having an open mouth, is to close it on something solid.'

G. K. CHESTERTON

⁂ praying in tongues ⁂

The walls of the Convent of the Pater Noster, built on the site on the Mount of Olives outside Jerusalem where Jesus is believed to have taught his disciples the Lord's Prayer, are decorated with 140 ceramic tiles, each one inscribed with the Lord's Prayer in a different language. This gives us the opportunity to create a multilingual version of the prayer, each line taken from one of the tiles.

Papa nou ki nan sièl la (Creole)	Our Father who art in heaven,
Qualtilia nite titukey (Aztec)	Hallowed be thy name.
Venha o teu reino (Portuguese)	Thy kingdom come.
Gwneler dy ewyllys (Welsh)	Thy will be done in earth,
Kia rite ano ki to te rangi (Maori)	As it is in heaven.
Dacci oggi il nostro pane quotidiano (Italian)	Give us this day our daily bread.
Forgie us the wrangs we hae wrocht (Scots)	And forgive us our trespasses,
Kâ arî mçs piedodam saviem parâdniekiem (Latvian)	As we forgive them that trespass against us
En leid ons niet in bekoring (Dutch)	And lead us not into temptation,
Mas deliura-nos del mal (Occitan)	But deliver us from evil.
Amiin (Wolof)	Amen.

ACKNOWLEDGEMENTS AND THANKS

*'If the only prayer you ever say in your life is
"Thank you", that would suffice.'*

MEISTER ECKHART

Thank you to the following sources:

Almost Catholic, John Sweeney, Jossey-Bass, 2008; *The Amazing Book of Bible Facts*, Martin Manser, Marshall Pickering, 1990; *The Bloke's Bible*, Dave Hopwod, Authentic Media, 2006; *The Book of Common Prayer*, The Church of England, Cambridge, 1662; *The Church Explorer's Handbook*, Clive Fewins, Canterbury Press Norwich, 2005; *The Cockney Bible*, Mike Coles, Bible Reading Fellowship, 2001; *The Complete Idiot's Guide to the Gnostic Gospels*, J. Michael Matkin, Alpha Books, 2005; *The Concise Oxford Dictionary of Quotations*, edited by Angela Partington, Oxford University Press, 1998; *The Daily Telegraph Book of Hymns*, Ian Bradley, Continuum, 2005; *The Diet of John the Baptist*, James A. Kelhoffer, Mohr Siebeck, 2005; *Gargoyles, Chimeres and the Grotesque in French Gothic Sculpture*, Lester Burbank Bridaham, Architectural Book Publishing Co., 1930 (republished by Dover, 2006); *A Glasgow Bible*, Jamie Stuart, Saint Andrew Press, 1997; *Harris's Guide to Churches and Cathedrals*, Brian L. Harris, Ebury Press, 2006; *The Holy Bible (King James Version)*, Odhams Press Ltd, 1932; *How to Read a Church*, Richard Taylor, Rider Books; *I Never Knew That was in the Bible!*, edited by Martin Manser, Thomas Nelson, 1999; *The Limerick Bible*, Peter Wallis, Verité CM, 2005; *The NIV Study Bible (New International Version)*, International Bible Society, Hodder & Stoughton, 1985; *The Oxford Dictionary of the Christian Church*, edited by F. L. Cross, Oxford University Press, 1958; *Pilgrimage from the Ganges to Graceland: An Encyclopedia*, Linda Kay Davidson and David M. Gitlitz, ABC-CLIO, 2002; *Teach Yourself Christianity*, John Young, Teach Yourself Books, 1996; *They Built on Rock*, Diana Leatham, Hodder & Stoughton, 1948, 1999; *A Treasury of Christian Wisdom*, edited by Tony Castle, Hodder & Stoughton, 2001; *The World Almanac and Book of Facts*, World Almanac Books, 2008.

www.adherents.com
www.apostles.com
www.babynamesworld.com
www.bbc.co.uk
www.bible-history.com
www.catholic.org
www.catholicdoors.com
www.chetday.com
www.christiananswers.net
www.christusrex.org
www.cofe.anglican.org
www.crivoice.org
www.cyberhymnal.org
www.dumblaws.com
www.gotquestions.org
www.imdb.com
www.newadvent.org
www.new-life.net
www.nmm.ac.uk
www.opendoorsuk.org.uk
www.religionfacts.com
www.sacred-texts.com
www.saints.sqpn.com
www.ship-of-fools.com
www.statistics.gov.uk
www.theonion.com
users.sa.chariot.net.au/~gmarts/index.html
www.wikipedia.org
www.wycliffe.org.

And thank you also to:

Elaine Moloney, for support, patience, suggestions and fact-checking; Helen Porter, for popes, proofreading and patron saints; Dene Kernohan and Sarah Heron, for sherry-tippling vicars; Katherine Venn, for wonderful support and editorial expertise; Wendy Grisham, whose idea it was in the first place; Jamie Hodder-Williams, for saying yes; Mark Read and Hennie Haworth, for a beautiful cover; Nick Fawcett for his sharp eye; Janette Revill for the text design; Brendan Walsh, for encouragement; June Gunden, of Peachtree; Andrea Waind, of the NHS Information Centre for health and social care; David Bilby of Wycliffe; Fred Slack and Gill Hooper of IBS-STL; the staff of the British Library; Sue and Willy Moloney, Ray and Beth Mills; Roben Mills, Anne Mills, Anthony and Susie Wraight and Elaine again, for giving me time and space to write; James Moloney and Hannah Moloney, for inspiration.